18096 EN
Zambia

Holmes, Timothy
ATOS BL 9.3
Points: 4.0

UG

ZAMBIA

Timothy Holmes

MARSHALL CAVENDISH
New York • London • Sydney

Reference edition published 1998 by
Marshall Cavendish Corporation
99 White Plains Road
Tarrytown
New York 10591

Originated and designed by
Times Books International, an imprint of
Times Editions Pte Ltd

Printed in Singapore

Library of Congress Cataloging-in-Publication Data:
Holmes, Timothy.
    Zambia / Timothy Holmes.
      p. cm.—(Cultures of the World)
    Includes bibliographical references and index.
    Summary: Describes the geography, history, government
economy, people, lifestyle, religion, language, arts, leisure,
festivals, and food of this high plateau country in the interior
of Africa.
    ISBN 0-7614-0694-8 (lib. bdg.)
    1. Zambia—Juvenile literature. [1. Zambia.] I. Title.
II. Series.
DT3042.H64   1998
968.94—dc21   97–22298
                        CIP
                        AC

INTRODUCTION

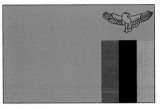

ZAMBIA, A HIGH PLATEAU COUNTRY lying far in the interior of Africa, has been mining territory for many centuries. But Zambia is more than mining. It is a large land of expansive panoramas where the main differences of scenery are between dry land and the many lakes and waterways. The greatest contrasts are among the people, some living in the sophistication of modern cities and enjoying the facilities of the technological age, others eking out an existence as subsistence farmers in almost inaccessible places. Before European colonization the people governed themselves in kingdoms, chieftaincies, or village groups. The present nation was formed by the mixing of peoples from all parts of the country around Zambia's copper mining industry, which propelled the society into the modern world. But the industrial areas cover only a small part of Zambia. The rest contains unspoiled natural wonders, among them some of the finest national wildlife parks in the world.

CONTENTS

A Zambian child wearing an amulet.

3 INTRODUCTION

7 GEOGRAPHY
Land of lakes and rivers • Climate • Vegetation • Animal life • Environmental concerns • The cities

19 HISTORY
The Stone Age • Iron Age immigrants • The kingdoms • The outside world moves in • Christian missionaries • Colonial rule • Federation • Independence • The one-party state

31 GOVERNMENT
Making the constitution • Human rights balance sheet • Political parties • Civic organizations • International relations • Defense and security

39 ECONOMY
Energy • Mining • Agriculture • Manufacturing • Transportation and communication • Trade and finance • Tourism

49 ZAMBIANS
Population • Ethnic groups • Minorities • Social stratification

57 LIFESTYLE
Birth, childhood, initiation • Marriage • Death • Rural living • Urban living • Zambian women • Schools and students • Social problems

CONTENTS

71 RELIGION
Traditional religion • Christianity • Islam and other faiths

77 LANGUAGE
Official and semiofficial languages • The language family • Writing • Language and education

83 ARTS
Literature and drama • Crafts • Visual arts • Music and dance

93 LEISURE
Popular sports • Relaxing • Children's recreation

103 FESTIVALS
Kuomboka • Likumbi lya Mize • Mutomboko • N'cwala • Shimunenga

113 FOOD
Women and food • Zambian specialities • Markets and supermarkets • Beverages • Dining out in Lusaka • Traditions and etiquette

122 MAP OF ZAMBIA

124 QUICK NOTES

125 GLOSSARY

126 BIBLIOGRAPHY

126 INDEX

A shawl secures the sleeping child as her mother works in the field.

GEOGRAPHY

ZAMBIA IS A LARGE COUNTRY shaped like a butterfly spread across the plateau of south-central Africa. It is 250,000 square miles (750,000 square km) in extent, which makes it the size of Spain and Portugal combined, or twice that of Vietnam. Zambia is landlocked, the coasts of the Indian and Atlantic oceans being some 600 miles (1,000 km) from its nearest borders. It is surrounded by Zimbabwe, Botswana, and Namibia to the south, Tanzania, Malawi, and Mozambique to the east, the Democratic Republic of Congo to the north, and Angola to the west.

The Zambian plateau lies about 3,000 feet (1,000 m) above sea level. There are no real mountains, but the highest part of the country, the Nyika plateau, rises above 7,000 feet (2,300 m). The most distinctive features of the landscape are the deep gorges and valleys of the lower Zambezi and Luangwa rivers. Their precipitous escarpments look like mountains from below. These troughs are limbs of the Great African Rift Valley, which extends from Mozambique to the Red Sea.

LAND OF LAKES AND RIVERS

In the far north of Zambia, the Rift Valley contains Lake Tanganyika, over 400 miles (650 km) long and 24 miles (40 km) wide. Only a small part of the lake lies in Zambia. The lake area is a place of indescribable beauty, attracting visitors from around the world.

Zambia takes its name from the magnificent river, Zambezi, which rises in the northwest corner of the country, then travels 1,700 miles (2,750 km) to its mouth on the Indian Ocean in Mozambique. The first third of its

Zambezi River (*above*) and Victoria Falls (*opposite*). The Zambezi hurls itself over the Victoria Falls, more than a mile (1.6 km) wide and as deep as a 30-story building.

Elephant herd in South Luangwa National Park. The Luangwa valley contains national parks renowned for their great herds of elephants and many other species of wildlife. Along the Kafue lies Zambia's largest national park, which is half the area of Taiwan.

journey is across a wide plain that floods at the end of the rainy season. Further downstream the river's gorge is blocked by a high dam to form Lake Kariba. Two hydro-power stations supply electricity to Zambia and Zimbabwe. The Zambezi is joined by the Kafue River, likewise dammed for electricity, and then the Luangwa, before flowing into Mozambique.

In northern Zambia the largest river is the Chambeshi. It rises near the Tanzania border, flows into Lake Bangweulu and its surrounding wetlands and emerges with a new name, Luapula. It feeds into Lake Mweru, emerges renamed Lualaba, which downstream becomes the Congo, and flows into the Atlantic Ocean. North-flowing rivers in Zambia flow to the Atlantic, south-flowing to the Indian Ocean.

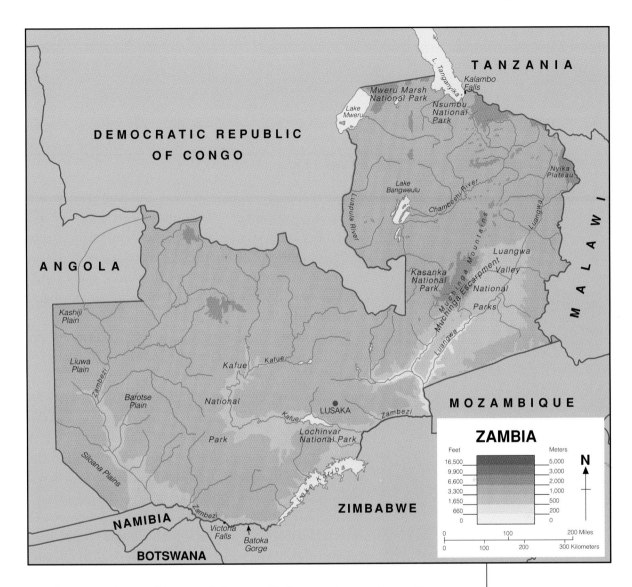

There are beautiful waterfalls on all the northern rivers. The most spectacular is Kalambo Falls, which drops an unbroken 300 feet (90 m) over the Lake Tanganyika escarpment. Many of Zambia's waterfalls have been declared national monuments, which means that they and their environs are protected from human defacement. In traditional religion they are believed to be the abode of the spirits of the ancestors, but this has not prevented some of them being used to generate electricity.

Forests cover an extensive part of Zambia. They appear uniform from afar but contain hundreds of species of trees which, in the high rainfall areas, reach great size.

CLIMATE

All the rivers mentioned rise on Zambian soil, which indicates good rainfall. The country does in fact enjoy a favorable rainfall pattern, though there can be disastrous droughts, most notably in the 1930s and the early 1990s. Precipitation is highest in the north with 50 inches (127 cm) per year, decreasing toward the south to as little as 16 inches (41 cm).

The rainy season, the equivalent of the Asian monsoon, starts around the end of October and lasts until March or April. The rest of the year can be totally dry, with clear blue skies day after day. Rain is, of course, vital for agriculture but has an extra significance for Zambia where more than 90% of all electricity is produced by hydro-power. The droughts of the early 1990s left the water level in the Kariba and Kafue dams so low that it was only a few inches above the intake of the generators.

Zambia lies between 8° and 18° south of the equator and is thus a tropical land. But the elevation of the plateau above sea level gives the country a largely mild climate, the temperature rarely rising above 95°F (35°C). The deep valleys, however, are much warmer, up to 105°F (40°C) or more. The hottest and most unpleasant period is the month and a half before the onset of the rains, when people can get very bad-tempered. The first thunderstorms bring relief and refreshment. During the short winter, from June to August, there can be frost on the plateau.

In a poll taken among foreign diplomats in 1996, Lusaka was voted the capital city with the most pleasant climate worldwide.

VEGETATION

Most of Zambia is covered by savannah woodland, open forest which varies in height and density according to rainfall and soil conditions. In the drier low-lying valleys the tree cover is much more open. Palms and the enormous fantastic baobab are common. Where the forest is crisscrossed by drainage lines the land is suitable for agriculture, while the open plains of the Kafue and Upper Zambezi rivers provide excellent grazing for cattle.

Where the forest has been cleared for farming it is possible to see clearly the great number and size, sometimes as large as a cottage, of the "anthills" built by termites. The termitaria carry their own unique vegetation and during the rainy season sprout edible mushrooms; one type has a cap a yard in diameter, making it the largest mushroom in the world.

Although trees have to be removed to make way for agriculture, industry, and human settlement, extensive areas have been set aside as forest reserves. In the national parks the natural vegetation from the tallest trees to the smallest flowers are as much protected as the wildlife.

The baobab, sometimes called the upside-down tree because its branches look like roots, reaches such a girth that it is possible to make a dwelling in its hollow trunk.

Around Zambia's built-up areas, natural forest removed for timber or fuel has sometimes been replaced with plantations of eucalyptus and species of pine.

Impala in the South Luangwa National Park, which is home to more species of wildlife than any other park in Africa, perhaps the world.

All the fish in a section of the Kafue River have been killed by effluent from a state-owned fertilizer factory, and other waterways in industrial areas are badly polluted.

ANIMAL LIFE

Zambia has a multitude of species living in their natural habitats. Eighteen national parks have been set aside to conserve different ecologies and their wildlife. For example, the Kasanka Park adjoining the Lake Bangweulu wetlands is conserving two rare antelopes, the black lechwe and the sitatunga whose webbed feet enables it to live in the swamps. The Lochinvar Park in the south is the home of thousands of red lechwe, a long-horned antelope adapted to life on a floodplain, and more than 400 species of birds, especially waterfowl such as pelicans, spoonbills, and the huge Goliath heron. Other notable birds along the waterways are the African fish eagle and the Maribou stork, which nests in the cliffs of the Kalambo Falls. Migrants from the northern hemisphere visit during the rainy season and bring the number of bird species recorded in Zambia to 699.

The incredibly varied fish life of Lake Tanganyika is conserved in the marine extension of the Nsumbu National Park. The lake contains over 600 species, many of which are unique, having evolved in isolation. These include hundreds of species of iridescent cichlids, and two species of the sardine-like *kapenta* ("kah-paint-ah"), which have been successfully transplanted to Lake Kariba. The largest fish in the lake are the giant catfish (200 lb/90 kg), Nile perch (130 lb/60 kg), and the Goliath tiger fish (50 lb/23 kg).

The Kafue and Luangwa parks abound in big game, with thousands of elephants, buffaloes, and large antelopes such as sable, roan, eland, and kudu. Lions and leopards are there too, and in Luangwa, a unique species of giraffe. Unfortunately, the rhinoceros is all but extinct, slaughtered by poachers to satisfy the market for its horn in east Asia, and the elephant is under constant threat for its ivory.

ENVIRONMENTAL CONCERNS

One reason Zambia has much of the natural environment intact is that it is a highly urbanized country by African standards, the rural areas being sparsely populated. In the cities, though, one finds all the pollution associated with industrialization. Many people living in and around cities have no access to electricity and rely on charcoal for fuel. Tree-cutting to supply this need is a serious environmental problem as thousands of acres of forest are destroyed each year, leading to soil erosion, the drying up of streams, and possibly a decrease in rainfall.

Zambia's generation of electricity from hydro-power is not a polluting agent in itself, but can result in environmental damage, as has happened at the Victoria Falls, where generators were installed half a century ago. People today are aware of the issue. A project that would have drowned

Agriculture can be a pollutant, too, and pesticides entering the food chain of the fish eagle (*above*) around Lake Kariba have caused a great reduction in its numbers there.

The population of Zambia's cities far exceeds the numbers they were planned for. Few enjoy the amenities of developed urban life.

the spectacular Batoka gorge (a miniature Grand Canyon) below the Victoria Falls on the Zambezi has been abandoned by the governments of Zambia and Zimbabwe, following protests by the chief of the Leya people who inhabit the area, supported by public opinion. A different site for the project, which will suffer little or no degradation, has since been selected.

Zambia now has an Environmental Council with strong legal backing, but it faces a huge task in getting industry and the mines to clear up the mess made in the past, and to make the cities with their inadequate water, sewerage, and garbage disposal systems more congenial places to live in. And until the people who inhabit them are able to afford electricity, charcoal burning will continue to destroy the forests.

THE CITIES

The small capitals of the king (Litunga) of the Lozi on the Upper Zambezi and of the king (Mwata Kazembe) of the Lunda on the Luapula River give an idea of what a pre-colonial Zambian town would have been like.

Unlike African countries such as Ethiopia and Zimbabwe, Zambia does not have ancient cities, whether standing or in ruins, because until recently in historical time, Zambians were generally semi-nomadic, their rulers moving their seats of government from place to place at short intervals.

The country's present urban centers were all built over the past century. Their architecture and street plans are Western, and until shortly before Zambia's independence, were segregated on racial lines. On the Copperbelt, the towns started as mining camps, each close to a copper orebody. Kabwe, in the Central Province, was built adjacent to the old Broken Hill lead and zinc mine. Ndola and Kitwe, the largest cities on the Copperbelt, have populations of about a million, while Kabwe has a quarter million. They are all busy industrial and commercial centers, with the Copperbelt consuming over 75% of the electricity used in Zambia.

Livingstone, Zambia's first capital, and Lusaka, the present seat of government, have different origins from the mining centers.

A street in Kitwe, one of the cities on the Copperbelt.

LUSAKA—FROM RAILWAY SIDING TO MODERN CAPITAL In the early years of the 20th century, Lusaka started its existence as a railway siding named after the local chief, a famous elephant hunter, and grew to be the commercial center for White farmers in the district. In 1932 the colonial government made it the capital of Northern Rhodesia because of its central position on the territory, and planned it on the pattern of an English "garden city." Buildings such as the present State House, the High

Stanley House and the Capitol in Livingstone. Like many buildings in Zambia's cities, these were built in the colonial period.

Court, and the Secretariat, were erected at this time, followed by the impressive Anglican Cathedral. At independence in 1964, the imposing National Assembly, with its copper roof, the University of Zambia, the International Airport terminal, and many more state and commercial buildings joined the skyline.

Lusaka was planned for 200,000, but today it has a population exceeding a million and a half, living mostly in poor conditions. But from its beginnings as a small outpost of the British empire, it has transformed itself into the hub of Zambia, and also of Central Africa, with highway, air, or rail links to the four points of the compass. Lusaka also has the distinction of being the only city in tropical Africa to be serviced by a commuter railway.

LIVINGSTONE—COLONIAL AND PREHISTORIC HERITAGE

What is now the city of Livingstone, built as a commercial center on high ground overlooking the Victoria Falls, was established when the railway from South Africa crossed the Zambezi on the bridge just below the Falls in 1904. The town was soon made the capital of British Northern Rhodesia, today's Zambia, the site being granted to the colonial authorities by the king of the Lozi, in whose territory it lay. It takes its name from the Scottish explorer and missionary, Dr. David Livingstone, who in 1855 gave the great waterfall its English name, which is used in Zambia alongside its original name—Mosi Oa Tunya, or "The Smoke That Thunders."

In 1935, Lusaka replaced Livingstone as capital, but it remains a place of great historical interest, apart from being beside the Falls. Zambia's national museum, the Livingstone Museum, and an open archeological site, the Field Museum, next to the Falls, show the development of *homo sapiens* in the area from the early Stone Age to the present—250,000 years of human history.

The early colonial buildings of the town give a glimpse of the more recent past, while the Railway Museum (above) holds a fine collection of locomotives and rolling stock from the age of steam. For these and other reasons, not least the Falls, Livingstone is known as the Tourist Capital of Zambia.

HISTORY

ZAMBIA'S FRONTIERS WERE DRAWN on the map of Africa a century ago by European imperial powers and it is thus a relatively new country. But it has been inhabited by humans and their predecessors for a quarter of a million years, as the archeological record shows. The skull of Broken Hill Man (now in the British Museum, London), found near the Kabwe lead and zinc mine in 1921, is of a person of the Neanderthal type, people who made stone tools and lived by hunting and gathering.

Bola Stone

THE STONE AGE

From about 15,000 years ago, during the late Stone Age, people had become modern humans, making sophisticated tools and decorating their rock shelters with pictures. These are the ancestors of the present-day San (Bushmen) of southern Africa, a few of whom are still found in Zambia. They were of small stature and lived in family groups, following the herds of migratory antelopes they hunted. They also ate tubers, wild fruit, and honey gathered from the wild, but did not grow crops, keep livestock, or construct dwellings. Skeletons found at one of their sites, beside a hot spring in southern Zambia, show that they suffered from tooth decay—too much honey, perhaps?

One of their hunting weapons was similar to the South American *bolas*, stone spheres tied to the ends of a rope which when thrown brought an antelope down by entangling its legs. These people are thought to have held the eland, the largest of African antelopes, as sacred (a surviving Zambian rock painting depicts this animal). The San lived in Zambia for thousands of years, but were eventually superseded by a different people who started arriving more than sixteen hundred years ago.

Above: **A spherical weight from a *bolas*. A pair of these, tied to the ends of a string, when thrown parallel to the ground by an expert thrower, wrap themselves around the legs of a quarry, causing it to fall.**

Opposite: **The Victoria Falls Bridge over the Zambezi, which forms the border between Zambia (once Northern Rhodesia) and Zimbabwe (Southern Rhodesia).**

The smelting of iron or copper was regarded as a mystic act. Copper cast in the form of a cross was used as currency.

IRON AGE IMMIGRANTS

About the fourth century A.D., people who made and used iron, kept livestock, grew crops, and lived in buildings had begun to occupy Zambia from the north. They formed part of the slow migration of tall, dark-skinned people originating, it is believed, in the east of modern Nigeria. Over a period of more than a thousand years they took over nearly all of Africa south of latitude 5° north. In parts of Zambia these negroid people displaced the Stone Age San; in others both lived side by side. The immigrants who, for convenience, are known as the Bantu ("bahn-too"), meaning people, were mining and smelting iron and copper 1,500 years ago, making weapons, fishhooks, and household items with the metals. They also made baked clay pots and beakers. About A.D. 1000 there was a further Bantu immigration, and the consequent admixture gave rise to the ancestors of the present Zambian people.

Meanwhile, in what is today southern Congo, to the north of Zambia, two Bantu groups, the Lunda and Luba, were developing into kingdoms.

Between A.D. 1500 and 1750 offshoots from these kingdoms moved into Zambia. They conquered all but the southern part of the territory and formed kingdoms of their own. Previously, Zambians had lived in small self-governing societies without a central political authority.

THE KINGDOMS

For a while some kingdoms in Zambia were subservient to the Lunda emperor, the Mwata Yamvo, but in time all became self-governing. In the north were the Bemba, ruled by the Chitimukulu; in the Luapula valley, breakaway Lunda, ruled by Mwata Kazembe; in the east the Maravi (ancestors of today's Chewa); and in the west, on the Upper Zambezi, the Lozi, ruled by the Litunga. Each king made subjects of surrounding peoples so that their nominal territories, held together by patronage and tribute, were extensive.

In the first half of the 19th century, two new groups of conquerors arrived from the present Republic of South Africa. A host of Ngoni, led by Zongendaba, and another of Kololo, led by Sebitwane, entered eastern and western Zambia respectively across the Zambezi. The Ngoni, who spoke Zulu, established a kingdom under Mpezeni I among the conquered Chewa. The Kololo defeated and took over the Lozi kingdom. The Ngoni tried repeatedly to conquer the Bemba, without success, but secured their place permanently in eastern Zambia. The Kololo survived for only three decades. Weakened by malaria, to which they had no immunity, they were easily overthrown by the Lozi they had subjected.

Lubosi, later called Lewanika the First, the great pre-colonial king of the Lozi. The Lozi were defeated by the Kololo in the first half of the 19th century. Three decades later, they defeated the Kololo and restored their kingship.

A slave caravan on the road. The trade in ivory and slaves went hand in glove, as slaves were needed to carry the ivory to the coast.

THE OUTSIDE WORLD MOVES IN

The first contact between different peoples is often the result of trade. From the earliest times in the Zambian area of the African interior, there had been exchanges of goods between producers of different commodities, for instance between salt makers and metal workers, fishermen and makers of cloth. Some of this trade, especially if it dealt with valuables such as copper and ivory, would have reached the coast.

The eastern seaboard of Africa had, from the days of ancient Egypt, been part of a trading network that extended to south and southeast Asia, and later to China. In the time of the Zambian kingdoms, this trade was in the hands of the Swahili, Muslim Afro-Arabs living in city-states along the coast and on nearby islands. By A.D. 1400 people in Zambia on the Zambezi near Kariba were importing jewelry from Asia.

On the Atlantic coast, the Portuguese established trading ports in the 16th century. By 1850, their merchants had reached central Zambia. The Portuguese were also in Mozambique, having driven out the Swahili, with a trading town as far up the Zambezi as where it is joined by the Luangwa River. The Swahili of Zanzibar, too, were penetrating the interior, and by the mid-19th century one of their merchants had crossed Africa from the Indian Ocean to the Atlantic.

Zambia thus became involved with both the Portuguese and Swahili mercantile empires. Money was hardly used for trade. What the Zambian rulers wanted most was color-patterned cloth, jewelry, firearms, and distilled alcohol such as rum and cane spirit. In exchange, they bartered local products like beeswax, iron, and copper and the more valuable ivory, rhino horn, and slaves.

From the west coast, the Portuguese shipped the slaves to mines and sugar plantations in Brazil. Slaves taken to the east coast could find themselves as far from home as the Middle East, India, and China. Many millions of Africans suffered this fate. Domestic slavery was an accepted part of the Zambian social order and many kings took part in its natural extension, the slave trade, which was not suppressed until the 19th century ended.

CHRISTIAN MISSIONARIES

Slavery was abolished in the British empire during the 1830s, as a result, partly, of the moral crusade waged by Christian abolitionists such as William Wilberforce. One of his followers, a Scottish medical missionary named David Livingstone, started working in southern Africa in 1840. During a visit to King Sebitwane of the Kololo on the Zambezi in 1851 Livingstone saw the slave trade in operation and decided to end it. His

David Livingstone's motto was "Christianity, Commerce, and Civilization," and he was influenced in his thinking by the achievements of Sir Thomas Stamford Raffles and Sir James Brooke, raja of Sarawak.

Cecil Rhodes (1853–1902). The French missionaries Coillard and Dupont helped Rhodes to bring the territory, under the name Northern Rhodesia, into the British empire by the end of the 19th century.

plan was to establish settlements where slaves who were being exported would work at home and produce crops, particularly cotton, for sale in Britain.

Livingstone died in Zambia in 1863, without success in his venture, but his life and ideals inspired other missionaries. Two of the earliest of these were François Coillard, a French Protestant who opened a mission to the Lozi of the Upper Zambezi in 1884, and Henri Dupont, a French Catholic priest who did likewise among the Bemba in the north during the 1890s. They were followed by others, Protestant and Roman Catholic.

Meanwhile, believing that Zambia was rich in gold, the British South African mining magnate and avowed imperialist, Cecil John Rhodes, was seeking ways to colonize the country.

COLONIAL RULE

From the 1890s until 1923 the country was administered by Rhodes's British South Africa Company (BSAC) under a concession granted by Queen Victoria. Coillard had persuaded the Lozi Litunga, Lewanika, to sign a treaty with the BSAC, and Dupont engineered the submission of the Bemba. Other kings—Mpezeni of the Ngoni, and Mwata Kazembe of the Luapula Lunda—were overcome by force of arms. Soon the whole territory was under BSAC control and the present boundaries largely drawn.

Rhodes's dream of Zambian gold did not materialize, but large tracts of land were taken over for White settlers. Although the BSAC abolished slavery, Zambians were subjected to a system of forced labor intended to

Miners check the drilling angle before work begins.

supply manpower for the gold and diamond mines of South Africa. It was a new form of servitude. Direct British rule after the departure of the BSAC in 1923 was more benign, though the White settlers were highly privileged and racial discrimination became the law of the land.

During the 1920s the rich orebodies deep underground along the Copperbelt began to be exploited. Skilled White miners were brought in from South Africa and Britain, while the large, unskilled workforce needed for mining was drawn from all corners of Zambia. The Copperbelt became a melting pot in which a Zambian national identity was born out of the many groups that lived within the country's frontiers.

By the end of World War II, in which Zambian troops served with distinction in Burma, Zambia had become one of the world's top producers of refined copper. But Zambian workers in the mines suffered racial discrimination—the "color bar" that kept them in unskilled positions.

Speaking of Zambians, an early colonial official remarked, "What a pity that the only destiny that awaits these ingenious people is to become the servants of the White man."

A long line of women voters outside a polling station in Lusaka during the first general election for North Rhodesia, on January 22, 1964.

A trade union movement developed, while on the political front the voice of Zambian nationalism demanding an end to colonial rule was heard ever more loudly. The Mineworkers' Union was headed by Lawrence Katilungu while the nationalist leader was Harry Mwaanga Nkumbula, with his African National Congress (ANC) behind him.

FEDERATION

Another post-war development was the scheme by White settlers in Northern and Southern Rhodesia to consolidate their power by federating the two territories. Despite widespread opposition in Zambia, including from some Whites, Federation was imposed in 1953.

The Zambians' struggle against White supremacy and colonial rule gathered momentum. Nkumbula and his ANC seemed unequal to the task, and a new liberation movement, the United National Independence Party (UNIP), was formed in 1958. Its most energetic figures were Kenneth David Kaunda and Simon Mwansa Kapwepwe.

So effective was UNIP's campaigning that the Federation collapsed in 1963. Zambia became an independent republic a year later, on October 24, 1964, with Kaunda as president. As for Southern Rhodesia, the British government insisted it would remain a colony until White minority domination gave way to majority rule.

INDEPENDENCE

Zambia entered independence with sails full of wind. Copper prices were high and the economy was in good shape, promising the resources to correct the inequalities of the colonial past. Schools, colleges, and a university were built, and health services greatly improved. Free universal primary schooling was implemented, secondary school enrollment quadrupled, and adult illiteracy was tackled. Plans were drawn up to transform Zambia into a modern, industrialized state, with the economy run by Zambians, not foreign-owned mining houses. It was anticipated that agriculture would outstrip copper as the principal earner of hard currency.

Northern Rhodesia's pre-independence all-Black cabinet after being sworn in, with the governor of Northern Rhodesia, Sir Evelyn Hone (front, third from left), and F.M. Thomas, deputy governor. Kenneth Kaunda stands next to the governor; Simon Kapwepwe stands at the back.

President Kaunda at the Commonwealth Conference on June 8, 1977, with British Prime Minister James Callaghan.

Then, in November 1965, the dominant White population of Southern Rhodesia declared unilateral independence from Britain and Zambia was drawn into what would become the Southern Rhodesian liberation war.

Apart from the material damage Zambia suffered, its plans for economic development were thrown out of joint. In addition to the conflict between Black and White in Southern Rhodesia, Zambia was also affected by the wars against the Portuguese colonialists in Mozambique and Angola, by the struggle against apartheid in South Africa, and by the war against South African occupation in Namibia. These events could not fail to distract the Zambian government from domestic priorities and to divert resources to unproductive expenditure.

By 1975, the Portuguese had withdrawn from Africa, the Mozambique peace treaty being signed in Lusaka. But the war in Southern Rhodesia continued until 1980 (when the country was named Zimbabwe) and that in Namibia until 1990, while South Africa was not freed from apartheid until 1994.

THE ONE-PARTY STATE

Kaunda's one-party state was not, as one might suppose, introduced in 1972 as a government of national unity in the face of the wars under way in countries neighboring Zambia. It was an ideological concept designed to turn Zambia into an "African socialist" state.

Kaunda nationalized 80% of the economy, including the mining industry. The civil service, police, and defense forces were politicized, and an all-pervasive secret police force was created. Opponents were jailed, often for years, without trial, with many tortured and some murdered. The president, with his ideology called Humanism, became a dictator. Though officially a "participatory Democracy," the one-party state was as authoritarian as the rule of colonial governors and ancient kings before them had been. Corruption, inefficiency, maladministration, and nepotism ruined the economy and perverted civil society.

The country was saved from total collapse only when Kaunda was persuaded, partly by the donors upon which the economy was by then dependent, to restore democracy. Apart from an abortive military coup, in which no one was hurt, and sporadic rioting in which about 20 persons were gunned down, no widespread violence occurred.

Free elections were held in October 1991, Kaunda and his party, UNIP, being voted out of office by a wide margin. They were succeeded in government by Frederick Chiluba as president, heading the Movement for Multi-Party Democracy (MMD).

Frederick Chiluba was a trade union leader before he became president of Zambia in 1991. The trade union movement was particularly important to workers in the mining industry.

29

GOVERNMENT

ZAMBIA HAS FOUND the transition from one-party to democratic government both troubling and exhilarating. Troubling because Zambians have for ages been accustomed to authoritarian rule. The pre-colonial kings and chiefs were hardly democrats, nor were British governors or the one-party president. Exhilarating because people can now do things that were out of the question before, like debating hot issues in public, staging anti-government demonstrations, or taking a cabinet minister to court.

Dismantling the apparatus of the one-party state has been painful for some. One method used by the previous government to bolster its support was to create innumerable unproductive jobs in the civil service and state-owned enterprises for its supporters. Such employment ceased when the civil service was trimmed to an efficient size, and state companies—most notably Zambia Airways—have closed down or been sold to private investors who will run them as real businesses. There is a close connection in Zambia between politics and the government's economic policies, and every move is scrutinized closely. The public pounces on any sign of reversion to dictatorial ways by president, ministers, or state officials. People expect perfection, but there are many disappointments as democracy does not come ready-made like a mass-produced automobile.

Above: **All aboard for a political rally. In Zambia, political parties must be registered, and religious and ethnic parties are forbidden.**

Opposite: **Non-Aligned Summit Monument in Lusaka.**

Zambian experience has shown that an entrenched one-party dictatorship cannot be reformed; it has to be uprooted and replaced by new structures.

MAKING THE CONSTITUTION

Zambia is a republic with a presidential system of government, like France or the United States and unlike India or Germany where the head of state is non-executive. Since independence in 1964 the country has had three constitutions, the present state being known as the Third Republic.

The independence constitution negotiated by Zambia's nationalists and the colonial power was enacted by the British Parliament. It provided for universal adult suffrage, a directly elected executive president and a national assembly from whose members the president would appoint a cabinet. Freedom of association was enshrined, which meant that anyone could form a political party.

The first president was Kenneth Kaunda. His United National Independence Party had a majority in parliament, with Harry Nkumbula's African National Congress and a party representing mainly Whites in opposition.

For a few years Zambia enjoyed a multiparty democracy, but UNIP had always been intent on a one-party state, following Lenin in Russia and Kwame Nkrumah, the first president of Ghana and an influential figure in Africa's emancipation from colonialism. Kaunda appointed a constitutional review commission, which toured the country to assess opinion, and duly issued a report that broadly favored UNIP's plans, though its recommendation that a president should serve only two terms in office was rejected by Kaunda. After coming to an agreement with Nkumbula on sharing the spoils of office, ANC merged with UNIP, and the "One Party Participatory Democracy" was ushered in with Kaunda as president and a few ex-ANC members of parliament, but not Nkumbula, in the cabinet.

Under the constitution of the Second Republic, UNIP was the only party allowed. State and Party were amalgamated, with the party supreme and the cabinet subordinate to UNIP's central committee. Parliament became a rubber stamp, and members who expressed criticism or asked awkward questions were removed. A State of Emergency was permanently in force,

Harry Nkumbula is one of several political leaders in Zambia who started their career in the labor movement.

Each party that has been in power has introduced a constitution which suits itself.
No Zambian constitution has been mandated by a referendum.

so that citizens could enjoy only such rights as the president conceded. Radio, television, the press, and publishing were placed under state control.

By 1990 opposition to UNIP had become too widespread to suppress and Kaunda reluctantly agreed to a new constitution negotiated with the recently formed Movement for Multi-Party Democracy, which had the support of the Zambia Congress of Trade Unions. Civil liberties were restored and the Third Republic was born, with Chiluba and his party winning the elections.

The MMD had promised to review the constitution once again and appointed a commission, which included nominees of the opposition, to do so. The government accepted many of the commission's recommendations, and presented these to parliament as amendments to the Third Republic constitution. Parliament approved with a more than two-thirds majority, but many people were unhappy that the matter had not been put to a referendum. This constitution contains a strong bill of rights similar to that in the United States and entrenches the independence of the judiciary. The president may serve only two five-year terms. But it contains two provisions that are contentious. One is its declaration of Zambia as a Christian nation: many people, including prominent Christians, would prefer Zambia to be a secular state, with a clear separation between religion and politics. The second is the clause stating that only Zambian citizens whose parents are or were citizens of Zambia may become president. First generation citizens and those who cannot prove their parentage are thus unable to aspire to the highest office in the land. A large proportion of the population is affected by this clause.

Children at Kasisi orphanage in Lusaka. According to the constitution of the Third Republic, orphans who cannot prove their parentage are ineligible to be president.

The constitution is now law, but public debate on issues continues. The constitution-making process is by no means complete.

The National Assembly in Lusaka.

Like all governments, that of Zambia tends at times to exceed its constitutional powers and trample on civil liberties.

HUMAN RIGHTS BALANCE SHEET

The constitution of Zambia guarantees freedom of expression and assembly, gives all citizens equal rights before the law, forbids ethnic or religious discrimination, and provides that no person may be kept in custody for more than 48 hours before being brought before a court of law. In some areas, however, these guarantees have not been honored. For example, Zambia's two main newspapers and the national broadcasting corporation remain under state control. Editors and journalists who displease the government have been dismissed. Moreover, the president is empowered under legislation dating from the colonial period to ban any publication he dislikes, and the laws on obscenity have very wide scope. Freedom of assembly is restricted by a Public Order Act which demands police permits for public gatherings.

In what are defined as "serious" criminal cases, for instance murder or drug trafficking, the accused may not be granted bail, which is a detraction from the independence of the judiciary, while the "citizenship" clause in the constitution concerning the presidency is seen by many as containing the seeds of ethnic discrimination. However, there have been few gross abuses of human rights since the end of the one-party state. There are no political prisoners and the president may only sustain a state of emergency for seven days without the consent of parliament. A permanent, independent Human Rights Commission has been established, and a Police Complaints Commission is already in place. Zambian citizens are by and large as free as those of any well established democracy, and do not hesitate to go to court if they believe their rights are being infringed by the state.

POLITICAL PARTIES

Of the more than 30 registered political parties in Zambia, most are very small, and only four are represented in the national assembly. In the 1996 elections, in which there was a 59% turnout of voters, the MMD won 131 seats, the National Party 5, the Zambia Democratic Congress 2, the Agenda for Zambia 2, and independent candidates 11.

Although former president Kaunda's UNIP could have won at least 30 seats, it boycotted the elections on the grounds that they had been "rigged in advance," which was patently untrue. UNIP is today essentially a regional party, strongest in the Eastern Province, where Kaunda has family connections, and relies heavily on its leader's prestige. UNIP has stated that it wishes to restore its socialist "Humanism," if not the one-party state.

The MMD is the party of economic liberalization. It enjoys nationwide support, has a strong business element in its membership, and a solid following on the Copperbelt. The three small parties in parliament are based on the personalities of their leaders, while among the independents are UNIP members who defied their party's boycott. The brand new Lima party, which represents farmers (*lima* means "to cultivate"), came close to winning a few seats.

CIVIC ORGANIZATIONS

Zambians take a great interest in politics, described as the second national sport after soccer, but the country is also alive with non-political civic organizations.

The National Women's Lobby Group puts up billboards as part of its effort to promote the advance of women in public life.

35

LOCAL GOVERNMENT

Zambia is divided into nine provinces, each with an administrative structure headed by a deputy minister appointed from parliament by the president. The country is further subdivided into 49 districts, each governed to a limited extent by elected councils responsible for such services as roads, water, health and hygiene, markets, and trading licences. The councils, headed in the cities by an elected mayor and elsewhere by a chairperson, are supposed to finance themselves from rates and revenue from licences, but very few of them are able to do so and rely on support from the central government. This is a grave weakness in the democratic structure.

Most notable among non-political groups are the trade unions and churches. The voices of many professional bodies are authoritative: the government listens to them, even if it does not agree.

During election periods independent monitoring groups come to the fore, while several societies are engaged constantly in civic education and campaigns to promote awareness of civil rights and women's interests. Journalists have set up groups to protect and extend freedom of expression. Humanitarian organizations such as the Red Cross operate freely, while among business people international clubs such as the Rotary Club and the Lions are popular and active in charitable work. Chambers of Commerce and Industry, the National Farmers' Union, the Law Association, the Economics Association of Zambia, and other professional bodies comment regularly on the performance of the government.

INTERNATIONAL RELATIONS

Zambia is at peace with its neighbors and on friendly terms with all member states of the United Nations, except for Iraq and Iran with which the MMD government broke diplomatic relations because of alleged interference in Zambian affairs.

The economy cannot sustain the cost of worldwide diplomatic representation, but Zambia has ambassadors at the UN and in major world capitals including Tokyo, Washington, London, Brussels, Delhi, Bonn, Moscow, and Beijing. On its home continent, Zambia is represented in neighboring countries and in Kenya, Ethiopia, and North and West Africa. It has established diplomatic relations worldwide with many more countries than these.

Zambia is an active member of the UN, the Commonwealth, and the Organization of African Unity, and, on the economic front, of the Common Market for East and Southern Africa and the Southern African Development Conference, both of which pursue the aim of regional cooperation. For decades Zambia, with the help of the UN and other agencies, has provided a safe haven for refugees from strife in Congo, Angola, Mozambique, South Africa, Namibia, Zimbabwe, and more recently Rwanda.

DEFENSE AND SECURITY

Zambia has a small army and airforce but has never been to war except indirectly, as when the country was attacked by South Rhodesian and South African forces during the liberation struggle against White rule in those countries. In the 1970s and 1980s the Zambian government allowed African nationalist fighters from those countries to use Zambia as a base. Since then, Zambian troops have served with UN peacekeeping units in Rwanda, Angola, and Mozambique, but at home the defense forces are engaged largely in civil operations and are politically neutral. The Staff College in Lusaka has achieved distinction and accepts military officers from neighboring countries for training. There is no conscription and the armed forces are a professional body which women may join.

The Zambian Police Service is understaffed, underpaid, and under-equipped, and this is one of the factors accounting for Zambia's high crime rate.

POLICE AND COMMUNITY

The Zambia police, which was politicized under the one-party state, has been reorganized since 1991 for its role in a democracy and renamed Zambia Police Service, with emphasis on community policing. Women often achieve senior rank. In many areas the public has formed neighborhood watches, which provide logistical support to the police, a system that has helped control crime, especially robbery and automobile theft.

ECONOMY

ZAMBIA IS AMONG the 20 poorest countries in the world, though it possesses a wealth of resources. Its annual per capita income fell during the 1990s to about US$300. The country is burdened with a foreign debt of more than US$6 billion, built up under the one-party state when the government borrowed recklessly. Much of the money was spent on consumption, for instance food subsidies, rather than on investment. To make matters worse, nationalized industries such as the mines and those set up by the state were mismanaged. When the MMD took over in 1991 it found, besides the foreign debt, an empty treasury, a rapidly depreciating currency, and an annual inflation rate soaring to 300%.

Under the guidance of the World Bank and the International Monetary Fund, the new government began to implement a Structural Adjustment Program (SAP). Its main objectives were to control inflation and stabilize the currency by cutting government expenditure to the bone. The "cash budget" principle was introduced, the government spending no more than it collected in revenue. All subsidies were removed, fees were brought in for social services such as education and medical attention, a Value Added Tax was imposed on goods and services, and an autonomous Revenue Authority established to collect taxes and customs and excise dues. The foreign exchange market was liberalized so that the currency, the kwacha ("kwah-chah"), became convertible and traded at market value. Since 1991 its rate against the US dollar has fallen from 500 to 1,300 kwacha. Another SAP imperative is to replace the state-controlled economy by a market economy. By 1996, 140 government-owned companies had been closed down or sold to investors.

Above: **Copper sheets prepared for shipment. Privatization of Zambia Consolidated Copper Mines Limited began in 1997.**

Opposite: **A farm worker harvesting peas.**

Despite reforms, the economy will need support from international agencies for many years to come.

Kariba Dam has power stations on both the Zambian and Zimbabwean sides of the dam.

Zambia lies on one of the world's great mineral belts, stretching from Congo in the north to the goldfields of South Africa.

ENERGY

The basis for developing Zambian mining, industry, and much else is the availability of abundant, cheap electricity, most of which is produced, without pollution, by water power. The largest of these generating stations is Kariba, which came onstream in the early 1960s. The next largest is the Kafue project, whose capacity is to be doubled over the coming decade. There are smaller but economically important hydro-stations in central Zambia, near Kabwe, at the Victoria Falls, and in the north, one of which, near the Kundalila Falls, supplies the entire Eastern Province. Zambia has the capacity to export electricity to Zimbabwe, Botswana, Namibia, and South Africa. It is connected to the Congo power system, from which it imports electricity when drought affects domestic production.

Petroleum products are imported from the Middle East. Crude oil is delivered by pipeline from Dar es Salaam port to the refinery at Ndola.

MINING

Iron and copper have been mined in Zambia for close to 2,000 years, and the country as we know it today was defined by mining. Copper, smelted and cast into bars and crosses weighing up to 50 pounds (22.7 kg), was an important item of trade five centuries ago, and most of the existing copper mines in the country are on the sites of ancient surface workings.

The modern mining industry reached its peak in the early 1970s, when Zambia was among the world's top four producers of refined metal and the second largest producer of cobalt, which occurs in some of the copper orebodies. Other subsidiary metals are gold and selenium.

Today the mining industry's copper output is about half what it was at the peak, down from 800,000 to 400,000 tons. This is not because of a shortage of ore but results from the mismanagement the industry has suffered during the 25 years since it was placed under state control. The industry is now in the process of being sold to private investors who will have majority shareholdings in the companies into which the state conglomerate is being split.

Copper and cobalt have long been among Zambia's prime metals, followed by lead, zinc, gold, and manganese. A large deposit of nickel awaits exploitation and uranium, a small amount of which was once produced on the Copperbelt, can be found in several places. There are also large deposits of iron ore, but it has not been economically viable to develop them. Mining is not restricted to metals. There are significant reserves of gems, in particular world-class emerald, tourmaline, aquamarine, and amethyst. Coal is also mined, as well as industrial minerals like talc, marble, limestone, and glass-sand.

Copperbelt miners wait underground for transport to the surface. Some of the largest international mining corporations are providing the capital to mine the large copper and cobalt orebodies awaiting development.

The mining industry contributes over 90% to Zambia's export earnings.

A worker burns off the leaves of sugarcane before the harvest.

About 70% of Zambia's staple food grains are produced on small farms, where much of the work is done by women. Their reward is minimal, hence many migrate to urban areas.

AGRICULTURE

Less than 10% of Zambia's potentially arable land is under cultivation. Instead of being an importer, the country has the potential to be an important exporter of grain. Climate and soils make large areas of the country suitable for crops like corn, sorghum, soy beans, rice, groundnuts, cotton, and tobacco. Wheat, coffee, and tea do well under irrigation during the long dry season, and irrigation is also the basis of Zambia's most successful large-scale agricultural enterprise, the Nakambala sugar estate, owned by the recently privatized Zambia Sugar Company. It produces all the country's needs and exports to neighboring countries, the European Union, and the United States. Other export crops, most of which are sold in Europe, are cotton and tobacco, and on a small scale, vegetables, flowers, paprika, and coffee.

Cattle farming is of prime importance in regions free of the tsetse fly, which carries a deadly parasite. The fly does not occur on the plateau areas of southern and eastern Zambia or on the Upper Zambezi plains. From time immemorial cattle have been at the center of the lives of the people there. Today commercial ranches are also large producers of beef, some of which is exported. Dairy farms, located mainly near urban centers, produce an adequate supply of fresh milk, which by law must be pasteurized before sale, and there is a growing number of butter, cheese, and yogurt makers. Farmers also supply the cities but not necessarily the smaller provincial towns with chickens, eggs, pork, and fresh fruit and vegetables in abundance. But most farmers remain poor, and agriculture, particularly grain production, is not a success story.

OBSTACLES TO SUCCESSFUL AGRICULTURE

Political leaders have been saying since independence that agriculture must become Zambia's most important industry. Yet 33 years later the country does not have a reserve of grain sufficient to compensate for crop failure due to drought. The 1996–97 season, which had excellent rainfall, failed to produce the country's requirements for grain because the government neglected to ensure that fertilizer was available at planting time. Human error, not drought, is the cause of food deficits.

From 1964 until 1991 President Kaunda's government was concerned primarily with the need to keep the urban areas happy with cheap food. Consequently, farmers were compelled by law to sell their corn, the staple food, to the state and were paid fixed, uneconomic prices. As a result, masses of peasant farmers drifted to the towns, where they could buy corn for less than it cost them to grow it, thus making the problem worse as production declined.

Since 1991, the MMD's policy of liberalizing the grain market has caused confusion. Many peasant farmers were unable to sell their crop, and were then unable to obtain credit to finance the following season's production. If one adds to that the high interest rate on loans and the inefficient "free market" distribution of seed and fertilizer, it is not surprising that the situation is bad. After its victory in the 1996 elections, the MMD declared that agriculture was to be its top priority. It remains to be seen whether this commitment will be fulfilled. Policies thought up by urban politicians who know little about the needs of farmers, especially small-scale peasant farmers, are the greatest obstacle to a successful Zambian agriculture.

Recycled metal products being sold, an example of small-scale industry.

MANUFACTURING

The liberalization of the economy since the early 1990s has had a negative effect on many Zambian industries which had been protected from imports. Competition has affected manufacturers of textiles and clothing particularly harshly. A number of state-owned enterprises, including motor assembly, industrial and domestic ceramics, and dry-cell batteries, simply collapsed.

However, the industrial economy, now free of state control, which, for example, dictated prices, is in a position to flourish provided it updates its equipment, meets international standards of quality, and keeps its costs down. These conditions will be difficult to meet, though, as there is a shortage of investment capital and interest rates on credit are very high. Besides that, the domestic market is small. For many companies the surest way to success will be through exports. Zambia is an active member of two regional economic cooperation groupings covering eastern, central, and southern Africa and is pressing for a free trade agreement that will enlarge the market for Zambian products. Among industries that have established export markets are cement, refined sugar, glass, copper wire and cable, and mining explosives and equipment. New export products include jewelry, bottled lager, frozen chicken, and cheese.

The government has passed an Investment Act which gives generous incentives and tax breaks to industrialists. With Zambia's resource of electricity, metals, minerals, timber, and agricultural produce (cotton, for example), manufacturing can become a growth area of the economy, especially when foreign trade barriers are lifted.

TRANSPORTATION AND COMMUNICATION

Landlocked Zambia has two operating rail links to the sea. Zambia Railways connects the country to ports in Mozambique and South Africa, while the Tanzania-Zambia Railway carries freight and passengers to Dar es Salaam. A third line, the Benguela Railway through Angola, is at present closed, and a link through Malawi to Mozambique is incomplete.

International road transportation has become a booming business since South Africa came out of isolation with the end of apartheid. Much of its trade with Central African countries passes through Zambia. All of Zambia's road transport, except the Post Bus carrying mail and passengers, is in private hands, having previously been nationalized. In 1992 the state-owned Zambia Airways Corporation was declared bankrupt and liquidated. Its services on internal routes have been replaced by privately owned carriers, some of which also fly to neighboring countries. Long-haul flights from Lusaka International Airport are provided by South African Airways, British Airways, Air France, Aeroflot, and KLM, among others.

Zambia Railways was constructed during the colonial period and Tanzania-Zambia Railway, opened in the early 1970s, was designed, built, and financed by the People's Republic of China.

Zambia's highway network is centered on Lusaka, with freight and passenger services to all provinces.

Zambia contains a host of attractions and is a book that is just opening to vacationers from abroad. But at the same time the tourism authorities want to ensure that the environment of tourist resorts is not degraded and that local people are not exploited but will benefit from the industry.

Zambia's internal telecommunications system is best described as rudimentary (the telephone directory for the whole country is less than an inch thick), but cellular phones are being introduced and ZAMTEL is connected to the international satellite network.

TRADE AND FINANCE

With its central position in the region, Zambia is becoming a focus for international trade. The annual International Trade Fair at Ndola on the Copperbelt, and the Agricultural and Commercial Show in Lusaka attract exhibitors from all over the world.

Commerce has been facilitated by the liberalization of the Zambian money market. Currency can be changed with very few restrictions, and the illegal money merchants of the past have gone out of business. The banking system extends to all corners of the country, and apart from local finance houses, British, United States, Indian, and South African banks operate in Zambia. The recently opened Lusaka Stock Exchange has started well.

TOURISM

The government is eager for tourism to become a substantial earner of foreign exchange, but does not wish to control and dominate the industry. Instead it gives support through the National Tourist Board and participates with the private sector in the Tourism Council. State-owned hotels and national park lodges are being privatized and roads to tourist destinations improved. It is not a free-for-all market; Zambian citizens are favored in the issuing of operating licences.

Unlike Spain or Thailand with their beautiful coastlines and beaches, Zambia is not a country for mass tourism. What it wants to see is the

development of small-scale but excellent facilities that will enable visitors to enjoy Zambia's unique attractions at close hand.

Tour operators now have the challenge and opportunity to build on and extend the existing facilities. Victoria Falls, undoubtedly one of the wonders of the world, has been Zambia's main attraction for decades, and the South Luangwa National Park is famous for its walking tours during which visitors can experience the wildlife almost face to face. Facilities in this park, including lodges and small camps, are well developed, but there is wide scope for expansion here and in the many other parks. Lodges on the shore of Lake Tanganyika offer visitors the opportunity to enjoy the beauty of the place, and to go fishing for Nile perch and Goliath tiger fish. Water sports from yachting to water skiing are popular on Lake Kariba.

There is growing interest in historical tourism—following the journeys of Livingstone and steam locomotive trips from the Railway Museum, for example. And of great interest are the festivals of Zambian peoples, whose color and spectacle, music and dancing draw thousands of spectators.

Visitors to a safari lodge are provided with a guide and vehicle to observe elephants in the South Luangwa National Park.

ZAMBIANS

A COMMON ORIGIN IS CLAIMED by nearly all Zambians. North, south, east, and west, the legends of people who speak different but related languages tell of a migration from the ancient Lunda-Luba empire in what is today Congo. Some peoples speak of origins even further north, while the Ngoni and Lozi remember their South African heritage. Apart from recent immigrants from Europe and Asia, Zambia is a broadly homogenous nation, with little of the ethnic contrasts that characterize Ethiopia or India. Most people regard themselves as the subjects of various traditional rulers, but what Western journalists call "tribalism" only rarely leads to conflict. Overall loyalty goes to the national flag.

Nearly 50% of Zambians live in urban areas where everyone is in a social mix. What differences in lifestyle there are, are those between the rich and the poor, between city sophisticates and their rural brothers and sisters.

Opposite: **A villager home-ward bound with her load of beans.**

Left: **Are they Ngoni or Lozi, Chewa or Lunda? In the city it is impossible to tell the groups apart by appearance alone.**

Though belonging to a tribe may be irrelevant to an increasing number of urban Zambians, such as these women, the major-ity of Zambians owe some allegiance to a traditional ruler and probably have relatives and economic interests in rural areas.

POPULATION

In 1996 Zambia's population exceeded 9 million. Statistics for infant mortality (1.5%) and life expectancy (45 years) are unreliable as many people do not register births and deaths. The country has the highest rate of urbanization in tropical Africa. Internal migration started in earnest with the opening of mines less than a century ago, and is continuing, though government plans to resettle urban volunteers on rural farms may reverse the trend.

Zambians tend to have large families, both a cause and a compensation for high child mortality. A Planned Parenthood Association, supported by the government and donor agencies, is active (while opposed by some Christians and Muslims), and there is an ongoing campaign to raise awareness of HIV/AIDS, a disease sweeping fatally through all levels of society.

ETHNIC GROUPS

The colonial authorities, aided by missionaries, divided the inhabitants of Zambia into over 70 "tribes." "Divide and Rule" was a convenient policy for the imperial government not only in Zambia, and enabled it to control the population through the chiefs it installed and paid. Where a people did not have a chieftainship, the government created one. To this day a Zambian's tribe and chief are recorded on the national registration card wherever possible.

The major groups in Zambia are those owing loyalty to the successors of the pre-colonial kings. In the west are the Lozi under their Litunga, in the east the Chewa under paramount Chief Undi and the Ngoni under

Mpezeni. In the north are Mwata Kazembe's Lunda and Chitimukulu's Bemba; in the northwest Ishinde's Lunda, Ndungu's Luvale, and Kapijimpanga's Kaonde. The Batu-Batotwe (three peoples) of the south who speak variations of the Tonga language have no paramount chief. Other significant groups are Mambwe, Namwanga, Tumbuka, and Nsenga in the east, Chokwe and Luchazi (northwest), and Lenje and Soli (center).

City members of such groups travel long distances to attend ceremonies, and chiefs often tour urban areas to stay in touch with their subjects. Seeing people on a city street, it is not possible to classify them by group as in India, where Sikhs look different from Assamese. In fact, the only distinguishable Zambians are the few unassimilated Batwa (pygmies) and San (Bushmen). With most of the population, ethnicity is invisible. It is easier to recognize political or religious affiliation from party T-shirts, church uniforms, or Islamic robes.

Besides traditional loyalty, Zambians classify themselves by clan. Clans are thought to have originated during the period of migration from the north. A party of migrants would name itself after a significant event, an animal, or a feature of the landscape. Clan names are sometimes used as modern surnames, for example, Ngandu (Crocodile), Mvula (Rain), or Chulu (Anthill). All clan members, no matter what language they speak or how far apart they live, see themselves as belonging to one family whose members are expected to help each other. A Tonga "Elephant," for instance, is morally obliged to give help to a Kaonde "Elephant." Marriage between members of the same clan is regarded as incestuous and forbidden by custom. The clan system operates over much of Africa.

A chief among his subjects.

Most Zambians belong to a single ethnic group, the Bantu, but speak different languages, a similar situation to that of the Slavs, for example.

Despite their small numbers, the Zambian minorities are well represented in parliament, elected on individual merit and not as group members.

Clans that were once enemies have over the years transformed their aggression into a game. Called the "joking relationship," this allows for the exchange of insults and mockery of the most extreme kind until everyone collapses in laughter. A joking relationship exists between the Bemba and the Ngoni, who in the past were often at war. This ancient tradition may explain why Zambians are generally great talkers but reluctant fighters.

MINORITIES

There are three conspicuous ethnic minorities in Zambia. One is made up of persons of mixed blood—Afro-Europeans or Afro-Asians. They are full citizens of the republic but generally do not owe allegiance to a traditional ruler or belong to a clan. Among them are professional and business people, farmers, and skilled workers. During the colonial period they suffered racial discrimination and lived in segregated suburbs. Less than 50,000 in number, two persons of this group are today elected members of parliament.

THE ROLE OF TRADITIONAL RULERS

What may be called Zambian royalty does not exercise direct political power, and the constitution forbids traditional rulers from standing for election to parliament or local councils unless they first resign their thrones. The constitutional House of Chiefs, whose members are selected by the traditional rulers themselves, has high status, but is little more than an advisory body to which legislation is referred for comment.

However, kings and chiefs are revered by traditionists as the intermediaries between their subjects and the spirits of their ancestors, and ultimately with God. In the traditional areas—which is most of Zambia—it is the chief who allocates land and who may withdraw the allocation. This gives the ruler great day-to-day power. Even under the 1995 Lands Act, a person in the traditional areas may only obtain permanent title to land of his or her own with the chief's consent.

Chieftainship is hereditary, but a chief may only occupy his or her throne after receiving recognition from the president. Apart from their subjects' tribute, chiefs receive a salary from the government and their palaces are maintained at state expense.

The second group comprises persons confusingly called "Asians," whose forebears emigrated from the Indian subcontinent from the 1920s onward, mainly as small shopkeepers. Today they number about 40,000 and are a strong force in Zambia's business life, owning banks, real estate, and large trading houses as well as being prominent in the professions. There is sometimes friction between the majority of Zambians and the so-called Asians, not all of whom are citizens of the republic, and the Kaunda government tried to force them out of the retail trade. But the relationship between this group and the majority is mutually beneficial and four Asians are elected members of parliament.

Today there are probably less than 5,000 White permanent residents in Zambia, and probably no more than 10% of these are citizens. There is, however, a considerable transient White population, employed on work permits in business, agriculture, industry, and the mines. New legislation allows genuine investors to acquire resident's status and to buy land, so the number of Whites with a long-term stake in the country is increasing.

Many of the mainly South African or British Whites living in Zambia during the colonial era departed at independence, unable to accept African rule.

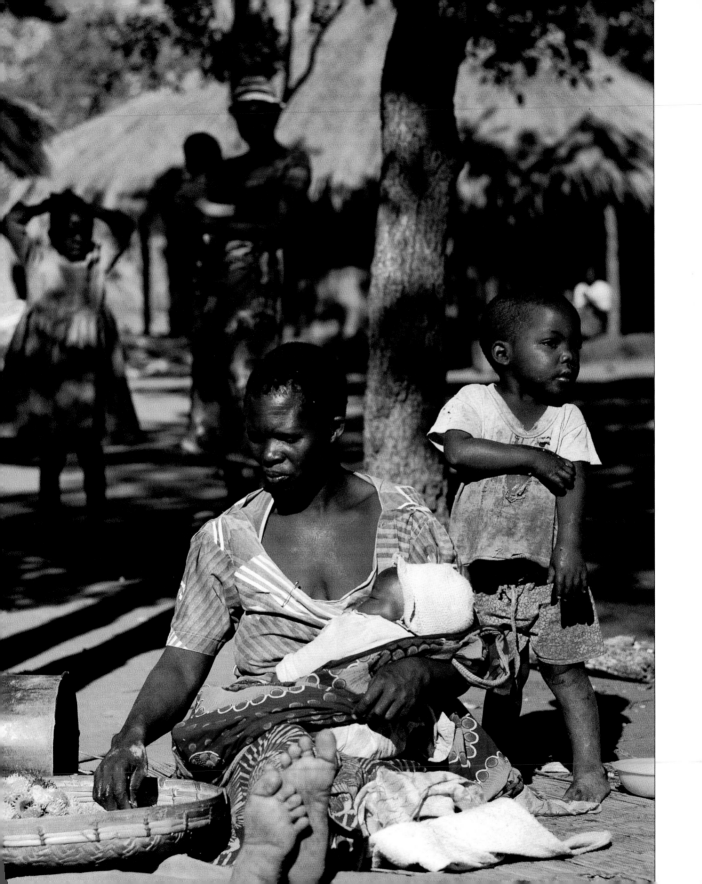

SOCIAL STRATIFICATION

In pre-colonial traditional communities the social structure was hierarchical. A typical example is provided by
the Soli, a people living to the east of Lusaka. According
to Soli historians, there were three classes.

The chieftainship was hereditary, with succession
through the female line. Only a member of a specific
clan, in this case the Beans clan, could be chief. He or
she had a council of advisors, often relatives, and their
position was also hereditary. Below the councillors were
the hereditary village headmen, who ruled the commoners on behalf of the chief. Chief, councillors, and
headmen constituted the ruling class. The villages were
usually family units, and the commoners were free
persons. At the bottom of the ladder were the slaves,
who, in the words of the historians, "provided free labor to the ruling
class." The slaves were mainly prisoners of war or criminals, but the poor
sometimes sold children they could not support into slavery.

In modern urban Zambia there is no hereditary ruling class, though one
of the reasons why Kaunda lost popular support was the suspicion that he
wanted to found a presidential dynasty.

Today's elite comprises those with wealth and political power which
enables a person to offer patronage and maintain a following. Except in
traditional society, wealth and power count for more than birth.

At the bottom of the social scale are the unskilled workers and the
unemployed. But this is not a rigid structure, and the extended family,
which is Zambia's basic social unit, may contain members of all classes.

Above and opposite: **Over
the past decade, Zambia's
population has been
growing faster than eco-
nomic development, and
many people are getting
poorer. This may mean a
greater disparity between
the upper classes of society—the university stu-
dent above, for instance—
and the majority.**

LIFESTYLE

AMONG ZAMBIANS, FAMILY TIES are a powerful force and the extended family is the keystone of the social structure.

Families are normally headed by a man, but many Zambian groups are matrilineal. In traditional society this means that when a husband dies his widow, children, and property are transferred to his mother's sister's eldest son. Today many an urban Zambian husband makes a will leaving his property to his widow, thus sidestepping the system, but disputes are common, and widows often find themselves stripped of their inheritance by relatives of the dead man.

Some men, including Christians, are polygamous, and it is generally true that in any marriage the wife's position is subordinate. These days many educated young women prefer to remain single, even when they have children. But though unmarried, they remain members of the extended family.

Broadly speaking, the extended family includes persons related by blood, who have obligations to each other, the richer helping the poorer and the aged being cared for. In Zambia it is very unusual, and considered disgraceful, for the aged to be placed in an old people's home.

Opposite: **Caring for a little brother or sister is a daily responsibility for women of all ages.**

Left: **Well-maintained town house.**

57

BIRTH, CHILDHOOD, INITIATION

Zambia has a high birthrate, and half the population is below the age of 16. In urban areas, expectant mothers can attend government antenatal clinics, give birth with medical attention, then receive help and advice from postnatal clinics. Rural areas have fewer facilities, and some of these are provided by mission hospitals. It is not unusual for a woman to have six or more children, though not all survive infancy. In traditional societies, children are treated as young adults as soon as they can perform tasks, when they care for younger siblings and help about the house and in the fields. These days youngsters start school at the age of 7, even earlier in the cities where there are many preschools run by the government and private individuals.

In traditional families, girls and boys undergo an initiation ceremony on reaching puberty. Girls are taught about sex and the duties of marriage by elder women. Boys' induction into manhood includes feats of endurance. After initiation, the graduates were ready for marriage. With the spread of Christianity and urban living, these practices are on the decline, but many adolescents are sexually active and teenage pregnancy often ruins a girl's education prospects.

Only one-third of Zambian children proceed from primary to secondary education, as there are not enough schools; also, schooling has to be paid for. This misfortune, together with general poverty, causes the growing problem of "street kids" in the urban areas.

MARRIAGE

There are two types of marriage in Zambia. Marriages performed by a civic registrar or a licensed priest or pastor are covered by statutory law. Succession to the widow is provided for, and the marriage can be dissolved only by the divorce court. Traditional or customary marriage is a contract according to the laws of the group, and the traditional status of the wife and the group's rules of succession prevail. The marriage may be dissolved in a customary court. Both types of marriage are less a contract between two individuals as between two families—they are an enlargement of the extended family.

Another factor in common is that the prospective husband is required to pay a bride price known as *lobola* ("lorh-borh-lah") to his future wife's family. It represents not the purchase of the bride but a pledge and compensation for lost services; it must be returned if the marriage is dissolved. Traditionally, lobola was paid in cattle or other livestock, but in urban Zambia payment in cash is common, and the parents of an educated woman may demand a high price. A high bride price may make it impossible for a man to marry the woman who has agreed to become his partner. The weddings of children of wealthy parents are elaborate and expensive affairs.

A wedding procession. It is usual for a Zambian bride-to-be to attend a bridal shower where she receives advice and gifts from the women-only gathering.

DEATH

As many members of the extended family as possible gather at the deceased's home. Every day at set hours, the Zambian radio broadcasts announcements of deaths, calling on relatives to come together. The deceased's widow or widower provides food and drink for the gathering, which may last several days before the burial. Among Christians, a church service is held. After the funeral, the mourners gather at the house. In some traditional societies it is then that the deceased's property is allocated, and the widow taken by her husband's maternal cousin.

In Zambia a funeral may last for several days. It is also usual to erect a tombstone at the grave a year after the death.

A vegetable plot supplies the family's needs as well as a little income. There is a great contrast between traditional peasant farms and the well capitalized, technologically advanced farming practised in the 5% of the country with permanent land tenure.

RURAL LIVING

Most land in the rural areas of Zambia is held under customary law. The chief is its custodian and the person who allocates it for use by his or her subjects. The people living in small villages are mostly farmers; some are traders and some government officials. Grain is grown during the rainy season, and pigs, goats, and chickens are kept, and sometimes cattle. Cotton and groundnuts are common cash crops, while near rivers and lakes, fishing is an important activity.

Many villagers live not much above subsistence level, producing enough food for themselves with a small surplus for sale, but nonetheless grow 70% of Zambia's grain. The main social characteristic of the rural areas is poverty. The Kaunda government attempted to improve matters by setting up collective and state farms, but these were a failure. Now new laws allow persons in chiefs' areas to obtain personal ownership of land, a move the present government hopes will enable farmers to get credit more easily and be able to produce more and become more prosperous.

A typical village consists of thatched brick or lath and plaster dwellings, with a meeting place, the *bwalo* ("bwah-lorh") at the center. Facilities such as schools and health centers may be a long distance away, and the roads are usually poor. During the rainy season some areas can be reached only by helicopter, and following a season of drought famine can become a reality in some places.

By contrast, the commercial farm lands held under private ownership mainly along the railway lines have a much more prosperous air about them. This area occupies about 5% of Zambia's land, and it is farmed largely by Whites, using modern technology such as irrigation and up-to-date machinery. With irrigation, two or even three crops can be harvested in one year. These farmers enjoy a comfortable, if not luxurious lifestyle, and their workers, though often poorly paid, are generally better off than the hoe and ox-plough cultivators of the more remote rural areas.

Rural women carrying home bundles of fuel.

Middle-income apartments close to modern amenities—one aspect of urban dwelling.

URBAN LIVING

The cities of Zambia cannot cope with the number of people who inhabit them. While vast tracts of the countryside appear empty of people, the urban areas, where some 50% of the population lives, are overcrowded and noisome.

While there is not a great difference in wealth between rural villagers, the cities exhibit the extremes—from the Hollywood-style mansions of the very rich to the squalid mud and plastic structures of shantytown dwellers and the street children sleeping in shop doorways. Between these extremes, the majority of citizens live in small houses in the townships (as the poorer suburbs are called), in apartment blocks, or dwellings they have built themselves in designated places provided with basic services such as water and sewerage.

Statisticians talk of high- and low-density areas, a euphemism for poor and rich, and it is only the latter that are adequately serviced by the city councils. In a high-density area within easy walking distance of a city center, people use pit latrines, draw water from polluted wells, and suffer outbreaks of dysentery and even cholera.

The richer areas, even if the roads are potholed, offer much that is available in developed countries—restaurants, five-star hotels, sparkling supermarkets, and video shops. A satellite dish adorns many a suburban garden, along with its swimming pool and tennis court.

But the cities, uncomfortable and filthy as they may be for the poor, are seen as places of opportunity. The drift into them continues, and will do so until the government implements policies that bring prosperity to the rural areas.

Shantytowns around the cities may be squalid, but they are seen by many as the first step into the modern economy.

ZAMBIAN WOMEN

Zambia has traditionally always been dominated by men. The presence of women chiefs and of the matriarchal system of succession did little to change the basic division of labor by which women were tied to work in the household and the fields. A woman's life was dedicated to producing and rearing children, producing and preparing food. Men did not have to endure this routine. They hunted, fought off enemies, and mined and smelted metals when necessary.

As in many other cultures, it is usually accepted that a wife must obey her husband, which is both a traditional and a religious habit. The missionaries started schools for girls, but the objective of this education was to produce competent housewives. Today, however, the Ministry of Education insists that there shall not be gender discrimination in the school syllabus.

Far fewer women then men complete secondary education, but positive measures are being introduced to correct the imbalance. For example, the government reserves 25% of its university bursaries for women, the remainder being competed for by men and women alike. Education and urbanization are working together to inspire women to make lives of their own.

TRAVELERS AND TRADERS

A woman travels hundreds of miles on the bus from the provincial town nearest her village to sell basketloads of mushrooms in the city. A woman makes a return train journey from Lusaka to Dar es Salaam, more than a thousand miles in each direction, and brings back items to sell that are not available in Zambia. A group of women on the Copperbelt find out from shopkeepers what goods their customers need and make a round trip by bus to get them in Johannesburg, South Africa. A woman flies to Bangkok and trades Zambian emeralds for the luxuries of Asia.

Zambian women's entrepreneurship is unquenchable and overcomes all obstacles, whether the arrogance of customs officers (usually male), the complications of Value Added Tax, or the fluctuating exchange rate of the Zambian currency, apart from the normal hazards of travel.

Although issues like the laws of succession have not been resolved to women's satisfaction, women may now open bank accounts and obtain credit without prior permission from a husband or male guardian.

Today there are women in all spheres of life—high court judges, ambassadors, doctors, lawyers, and in business. But the present cabinet contains only one woman minister out of 25 and fewer than 10% of members of parliament are female. Despite this, it is acknowledged that women are a component without which the modern Zambian economy could not operate and progress.

The traditional precept that a woman must be subject to her husband is accepted widely in Zambia, by men and some women themselves.

Opposite: **A working mother shucks corn to prepare a meal.**

Left: **Women entrepreneurs are found everywhere in Zambia where opportunity presents itself.**

Schoolchildren in Ndola. Zambians yearn for education, but though matters are improving under the new government, it will be a long time before the nation reaches the standards of Singapore or Cuba, to name two countries where education policies have succeeded over the past 30 years.

SCHOOLS AND STUDENTS

At independence there were only 120 Zambians with university degrees, and a mere 1,000 who had completed secondary education. It was only at that time that the mining companies started to recruit Zambians for skilled work.

A priority of the Kaunda government was the rapid extension of educational opportunities. Within a few years of independence secondary schools were built in all 47 districts of the country. Universal free primary education was introduced, and at the other end of the ladder, the University of Zambia was erected and opened in Lusaka. Technical colleges were expanded or established from scratch, and a University Teaching Hospital was built in Lusaka to train physicians. The Natural Resources Development College set about training for careers in agriculture, among other disciplines, and the National Institute for Public Administration prepared students for the civil service. Later, the Copperbelt University, dealing with technical subjects, opened at Kitwe.

Unfortunately, the government could not keep up the initial momentum in this field. By the 1980s much of the system was in decay. In 1997 only 16% of secondary school graduates who qualified for university could be accommodated, and probably no more than 50% of the adult population is functionally literate. The post-1991 government has established a program to rehabilitate schools (many of which at that time had no desks or window panes) and to pass their management from the Ministry of Education to school boards on which parents are represented. Schools are expected to become self-financing. Likewise, the University of Zambia and the Copperbelt University have been made autonomous.

Free education is a thing of the past, though government grants and scholarships are available. University and college students often engage in rowdy protests about the level of fees, while school teachers are often on strike for better salaries. In response to the inadequacies of the state education system, many privately owned primary and secondary schools as well as professional colleges have been established.

Zambia has about 520 intermediate and secondary schools. Female enrollment is only 56% that of male enrollment.

67

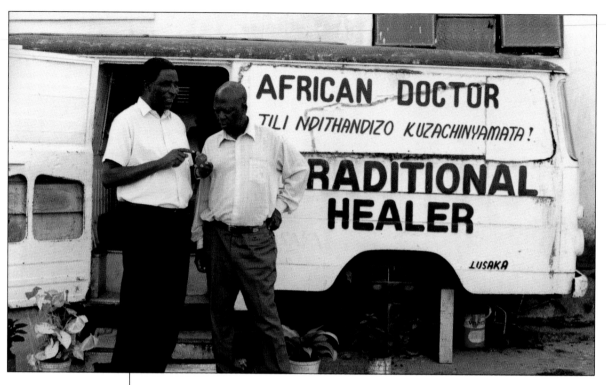

A traditional healer operates from a disused van in Lusaka.

SOCIAL PROBLEMS

HIV/AIDS The first cases of Acquired Immune-Deficiency Syndrome (AIDS) were positively diagnosed in Zambia in the early 1980s, although the disease is believed to have been present but unrecognized long before that. Today, AIDS is moving through the population like a plague. The most recent figures suggest that one in three post-adolescent persons is infected with the virus that causes the disease, and that 500 persons contract the infection every day. As there is no cure for the illness, the Ministry of Health and non-governmental organizations are campaigning vigorously to persuade people to change their sexual habits, since AIDS is most commonly transmitted during intercourse.

Many economically active persons are dying as a result of the disease, while the number of "AIDS orphans" far exceeds even the capacity of the generous extended family system to absorb. The main orphanage, run by nuns of the Catholic Church near Lusaka, is overwhelmed with parentless children, many of them infected with HIV themselves. Like tuberculosis

BE CAREFUL! YOUR FAMILY STILL NEEDS YOU!

STOP CASUAL SEX-PREVENT AIDS

NATIONAL AIDS PREVENTION AND CONTROL PROGRAMME-ZAMBIA

and syphilis in 19th century Europe, AIDS is a social disease that can only be brought under control when living standards improve and education makes the population aware of its cause and means of transmission.

CRIME Poverty, rapid urbanization, and the get-rich-quick ethic of crude capitalism have led to a burgeoning of crime in Zambia over the past decades. Robbery, car theft, and white-collar crime are commonplace. This is an issue Zambia could deal with itself if the country had not been drawn into the international trade in drugs. During the 1980s Zambia became a transit point for the drug mandrax, manufactured mainly in India, and with a big market in South Africa. Now Asian heroin and South American cocaine are passing through. An increasing number of young Zambians are becoming addicts. Under Zambian law, drug trafficking and activities associated with it carry severe penalties. The Drugs Enforcement Commission works to some effect with similar agencies worldwide, but Zambia's problem is only a small part of an international social disorder which seems immune to current methods of treatment.

RELIGION

THE PREAMBLE TO the present constitution declares Zambia to be a Christian nation, but does not make Christianity the state religion. The rights of adherents of other faiths are guaranteed. The president has appointed a deputy cabinet minister to act as intermediary between the Church and the State. It is doubtful whether the majority of Zambians are practising Christians.

There can be no doubt that Christians have made a deep impact on the development of Zambia, since it was the missionaries who introduced Western education. They were also in the forefront of the movement to suppress the slave trade in the 19th century, some of the first mission stations being refuges for liberated slaves. But thereafter missionaries worked hand in hand with the colonial government. Nearly all the leaders of the struggle for independence came out of mission schools. President Chiluba, like his predecessor, Kenneth Kaunda, is a practising Christian.

The declaration of Zambia as a Christian nation has not impinged on the freedom of other religions.

Opposite: **A church in rural Zambia.**

Left: **Old Mission Church near Kazembe in Luapula Province.**

TRADITIONAL RELIGION

When missionaries started work in what is today Zambia they found they were not preaching to godless people. Although it had no written texts, the traditional religion of people speaking the Bantu languages, as in much of Africa, was and still is a coherent system of belief. The supreme god, who goes by Lesa and other names, is the creator of the world and of everything in it. Mankind was at first created immortal, and later became subject to death, but human spirits lived on, intervening in human affairs and in relations with Lesa. The spirits are, therefore, honored and even worshiped as if they were demigods.

The living and the dead form part of a single community, joined together through certain individuals, notably the chiefs, who are in a sense also priests, and through mediums in some instances, who are entered and taken possession of by the spirits. The spirits can be either benign or evil, the latter being the source of power behind what Westerners call witchcraft, which brings disease, misfortune, and death.

Also included in this community is the land, the foundation of human life. It is thus that a chief's authority in allocating land has a spiritual as well as a political significance.

While a person's spirit lives on, there is no belief in reincarnation nor in punishment (hell) or reward (heaven) for behavior while the person is alive. Just desserts are suffered or enjoyed while on earth, and there is no notion of personal redemption or salvation. Lesa, as supreme god, is there, and does not direct human affairs like the Jewish and Christian Jehovah,

Near Ndola, a traditional healer treats a patient. In traditional Zambian religion, death was brought into the world by a reptile, the chameleon. In the scriptures followed by Jews, Christians, and Muslims alike, death was brought by another reptile, the serpent.

but in times of trouble, or to ward it off, the spirits may be appeased with offerings and sacrifices. Each household has its own spirits, and in several respects the religion of Lesa is similar to that of the ancient Romans.

A missionary visits a church member.

CHRISTIANITY

The 1990 census, the most recent, ignores religion in its statistics so it is not possible to say how many members any particular church embraces, but it is generally agreed that Roman Catholicism has the largest single following. The earliest missionaries in Zambia, however, were Protestants of the reformed churches, represented by the Paris Evangelical Missionary Society and the London Missionary Society, to which David Livingstone, the antecedent of all the missionaries, had belonged. Most of the reformed churches are now amalgamated in the United Church of Zambia. Other established denominations are the Anglicans, Presbyterians, Baptists, and the Salvation Army. There is a growing number of charismatic fundamentalist groups who take the Bible as literal truth, and the Unification Church of

Many Christian beliefs, especially those of Roman Catholics, can without much difficulty accommodate themselves to those of the monotheistic traditional religion of Zambia. The concept of saints and angels is close to that of the spirits.

A congregation at worship. Zambian Christianity is split into many denominations and sects, but is known collectively as "The Church."

Korean origin is also present. Eastern Christianity is represented by the Greek and Coptic Orthodox churches.

There are some Africanist sects, which fuse Christianity with traditional religion. A former Roman Catholic archbishop of Lusaka, Reverend Emmanuel Milingo, moved in this direction and practised spiritual healing. He was removed from his see by the Pope. Today the most noticeable Africanist church is that of the Zion Apostolics, whose bearded leaders, or prophets, like King Solomon of old, take many wives. A self-sufficient group originating in the suburb of Korsten, Port Elizabeth, South Africa, they were at first basketmakers, but now also proficient tinkers and metalworkers, and work communal farms. One of Lusaka's suburbs, Mandevu (meaning "beards"), is named after them. The church has branches all over central and southern Africa.

Of the mainstream churches, the Roman Catholic has gone farthest in Africanizing itself. Colorful ceremonials with drumming, singing, and dancing are part of its Zambian liturgy. This church in particular opposed the one-party state and was instrumental in its downfall when the bishops openly condemned its corruption and dictatorial practices. But today its total opposition to contraception and the recommended use of condoms as a precaution against HIV/AIDS is regarded by many as reactionary.

The fundamentalist groups, to which the president and several cabinet ministers belong, are influenced by the TV-evangelism emanating from the United States. They hold crusades and demonstrations of faith-healing, where in moments of high emotional pitch they invite people to be "born again" in Christ. Their members are known colloquially as "born agains."

Although there are many matters of doctrine and practice upon which the various churches disagree, they cooperate in producing a weekly Christian newspaper, the *National Mirror,* and sometimes work together on social projects. The larger denominations have schools, orphanages, and hospitals of their own which provide a most valuable service to the country as a whole.

ISLAM AND OTHER FAITHS

Islam was established in the city states of the East African coast 800 years ago, having been introduced by Arab and, some believe, Iranian traders. In the second half of the 19th century, Zanzibar was the principal city of the coast and merchants from there traveled into the interior of Central Africa, taking Islam with them. No large Muslim communities developed in Zambia from this source, perhaps because it was associated with the slave trade, though in Malawi, Zambia's eastern neighbor, many people were converted. Apart from a few Zambians, Muslims in the country today are mainly immigrants from the Indian subcontinent and their descendants.

A Hindu temple and a mosque side by side in Lusaka. In the past Islam has not been a proselytizing faith in Zambia, but the number of Zambian Muslims is increasing.

Mosques are prominent in the main urban centers, and the Muslim community is well known for its charitable work, which includes assistance to Christian hospitals. A newly opened Islamic Foundation near Lusaka offers welfare facilities and schooling to young Zambians, and its activities could lead to an increasing number of converts.

Zambia's "Asian" community also includes many Hindus. Other faiths include the Sikhs, the Baha'i, and a small number of Buddhists and Jews.

LANGUAGE

AS INDEPENDENCE APPROACHED Zambians engaged in a heated debate over the choice of an official language for the post-colonial state.

Pan-Africanists favored Swahili, the main language of Tanzania, Kenya, Uganda, and the Comoro Islands, and also spoken in parts of Congo, Mozambique, and Somalia, as well as in small areas in Zambia itself. Swahili had the advantage of being closely related to Zambian languages and of not being the tongue of any specific nation or group, having evolved along the African east coast in an interaction between local dialects and Arabic. The Pan-Africanist view was that by adopting Swahili, Zambia would be taking an important step toward the goal of African unity and replacing English with a language untainted by colonialism. Those favoring the retention of English argued that it was the most widely used international language. If it had been the tongue of foreign rule, that was now irrelevant. They added that Swahili had, in any case, been the language of Zanzibari slave traders who had wreaked havoc in the country before the British put a stop to their activities.

As things turned out, English was chosen. Swahili as an alternative has been largely forgotten, to the extent it is not even taught in schools or the university. The preferred second international language today is French.

Above: **Zambians in a rural setting speak the local dialect.**

Opposite: **Civic posters in Lusaka are in the official language.**

OFFICIAL AND SEMIOFFICIAL LANGUAGES

As the official language, English is used by all government offices and the police and defense forces. The constitution and all legislation is written and published in English, and hearings in the high court and the magistrates' courts are conducted in English, with translation when necessary through interpreters. The business of the national assembly is carried out in English, and candidates seeking election must by law show that they can use it proficiently. English is employed exclusively on two of the Broadcasting Corporation's three radio channels, and almost solely on television and in the press. It is the language of domestic and international business, and also the country's *lingua franca*, enabling persons with different mother tongues to communicate.

Seven local languages have semiofficial status: Bemba, Kaonde, Lozi, Lunda, Luvale, Nyanja, and Tonga. They are used in the local courts, which deal with litigation under customary or traditional law. They share one radio channel and have about an hour each on television every day.

Bemba, Kaonde, Lunda, Luvale, and Nyanja derive from the ancient Lunda-Luba empire. Tonga was brought by earlier arrivals from the north, while modern Lozi comes from the 19th century Sotho language of the Kololo invaders from the south. The other invaders from the south, the Ngoni, have lost their original Zulu tongue and now speak Nyanja.

Many Zambians are multilingual, and it is not unusual for a conversation to be carried on in several languages, including English, at the same time.

THE LANGUAGE FAMILY

The Zambian languages are members of the extensive family of Bantu languages spoken from southern Sudan in the north to South Africa, and include tongues as widely used as Swahili, Lingala (in Congo), and Zulu. The Bantu people are believed to have their roots in eastern Nigeria, and the languages are related to some of those in West Africa.

ZAMBIAN ENGLISH

English as used in Zambia has acquired some peculiarities, for example:

Butchery = Butcher's shop
Honda = Any motorcycle
Saladi = Any salad or cooking oil
Surf = Any washing powder
Vanette = Small pick-up truck
Beer = Any alcoholic drink, e.g. "Whisky is my favorite beer."

FOREIGN INFLUENCES

Zambian languages have absorbed and adapted words from outsiders, for example:

Bemba's *Citabu* ("chi-tah-boo") is from *kitab*, Swahili/Arabic for "book"
Nyanja's *Tirigo* ("tee-ree-goh") is from *trigo*, Portuguese for "wheat"
Nyanja's *Nsapato* ("in-sah-pah-too") is from *sapato*, Portuguese for "shoe"
Luvale's *Njanena* ("in-jah-nair-nah") is from *janela*, Portuguese for "window"
Nyanja's *Galimoto* ("gah-lee-morh-torh") is from the English "motorcar"

It is said in Zambia that a Lungu-speaking person from the shore of Lake Tanganyika who walks from village to village for 1,000 miles (1,600 km) to reach Victoria Falls will experience no difficulty with language as one dialect merges into its successor along the whole length of the route. Shortly after starting the journey, the hiker crosses Chambeshi River and ends the trip on the banks of the Zambezi—the names of both rivers mean the same: *cha* = *za* = big + *mbeshi* = *mbezi* = water. Big Water.

The way in which Bantu languages work is unique. The system is based on the root of the noun, and nouns fall into different classes, each bearing a specific prefix which is transferred to the verb and the adjective. To take two short hypothetical examples: the root *ntu* ("in-too") signifies an "essence," the prefix *mu* signifies "living." Thus *muntu* means "person" or "human being." The plural of *mu* is *ba*, so *bantu* means people. The prefix *i* signifies "inanimate." Thus *intu* means "thing" and *izintu*, "things." A sentence is held together by the prefixes, for example:

Izintu	*zonse*	*zanga*	*zagwa.*
Things	all	mine	are falling down.

The Bantu languages are the most alliterative in the world.

Despite the great distances that separate Bantu speakers, their languages have the same sort of grammar and share much vocabulary—in Swahili, Nyanja, and Zulu, for example, kufa *("koo-fah") means "to die."*

Above and below: **English is almost the only language of the press, but children are taught in one of the seven semiofficial Zambian languages for a few years in primary school.**

Foreigners wishing to learn Zambian languages can be frustrated by the lack of comprehensive grammars, dictionaries, and ordinary reading matter.

WRITING

Zambian languages were first put into writing by missionaries, who used the Roman alphabet. One of the earliest newspapers in Zambia, the French evangelicals' *Liseli* ("lee-sair-lee," the Pleiades) was published in Lozi in the early 20th century. Major parts of the Bible have been translated into Zambian languages, though the accuracy of a recent Bemba translation has been disputed. In the 1950s the government set up the African Literature bureau to prepare and publish texts in Zambian languages, laying the basis for non-religious literary works.

The recognition and semiofficial status of only seven languages is in fact a compromise, as there are more than that number in use, and some groups feel they have been left out. It is, however, difficult to draw the line between language and dialect, so it is likely the position will not be altered.

ZAMBIAN PROVERBS

Proverbs express succinctly the ethical codes and social relations of the people from whom they spring. Many are relevant to daily behavior, and proverbs from peoples as distant from each other as the English and the Bemba are sometimes startlingly similar. The following are from various Zambian groups.

Bemba	• A child that does not travel praises his mother as the best cook.
	• Those who eat iguanas are found close to each other.
Kaonde	• The mouth gets the head into trouble.
	• If you followed what a chicken eats, would you eat the chicken?
Lozi	• One finger cannot crush a louse.
	• A cow does not find its own horns heavy.
Luvale	• Firewood for cooking an elephant is gathered by the elephant itself.
	• The snake bites because its hole is blocked.
Nyanja	• The person who does not hear learns when the axe is in his head.
	• If you are ugly, know how to dance.
Tonga	• He who asks won't be poisoned by mushrooms.
	• Wisdom can come from even a small anthill.
	• It takes more than one day for an elephant to rot.

(Adapted slightly from *Zambian Proverbs* by Nyambe Sumbwa, published by ZTC Publications and Multimedia Publications, Lusaka, 1993. Copyright reserved.)

LANGUAGE AND EDUCATION

The first years of primary education are given in the semiofficial language predominating in the area: Bemba in the Northern Province, Nyanja in the Eastern Province and Lusaka. Disputes in the past over the boundaries of school language areas were settled by compromise. Beyond these years, English is the medium of instruction, with the Zambian languages studied as subjects. Where resources allow, French is introduced in secondary schools. English is the medium at the University of Zambia and the Copperbelt University. At present, English dominates in Zambian intellectual discourse and has without doubt helped to unite the nation across its linguistic divides, minor as they may be. On the other hand, it has been realized that Zambian languages must develop if they are to play their rightful role in the national culture.

The Alliance Française promotes French with evening classes, libraries, and cultural centers in several cities. Some foreign residents, such as the Italians, have schools of their own.

ARTS

THE TRADITIONAL ARTS of Zambia suffered severely during the colonial period. The crafts of the potter and the metalworker were driven almost to extinction by the import of factory-made goods, while music, song, and dance, being associated with rituals and ceremonials, were discouraged and in some instances forbidden by missionaries and the government. The missionary saw them as manifestations of a pagan culture that should be replaced by Christian civilization. From the government's standpoint, any form of artistic expression that mocked it or reminded people they had once ruled themselves was a threat to its authority. These arts were trivialized, stripped of their spiritual context, and turned into tourist entertainment.

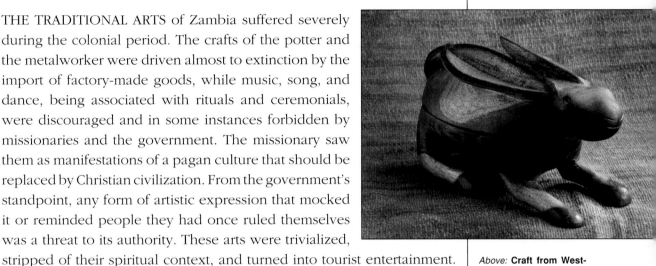

Above: **Craft from Western Province.**

Opposite: **A masked performer at the Maramba Cultural Village.**

Similarly, the people's oral tradition—the poetry and stories that formed an unwritten scripture of traditional religion—was ignored by missionaries unless it could be fitted into the Christian pattern of belief. The Bible, as interpreted by the Church, became the source of authority and truth.

The one-party state, which followed colonial rule, also inhibited artistic expression, insisting that it should conform to the Party's ideology. But Zambia's artistic spirit has proved irrepressible, and its need for support has led the new government to establish an autonomous arts council funded by parliament. It provides assistance to artists, painters, sculptors, writers, and performers, and these people have made it clear they will not tolerate political interference in the council's activities.

LITERATURE AND DRAMA

Zambian literature and drama have their roots in the storytelling, song, and dance of the traditional village, but there is little surviving record of this

in its authentic form. Even in recent decades very few literary works have been published, partly because of the high rates of illiteracy and poverty which restrict the market for books, and partly because until 1991 the only publishers in the country were either the state-owned Kenneth Kaunda Foundation or a firm belonging to the churches. Both kept imaginative poets and fiction writers under control.

A few novels in English have been published abroad, notably Dominic C. Mulaisho's *The Tongue is Dumb* (1968). Fiction in local languages has been largely confined to texts suitable for use in schools. A few biographies, such as Goodwin Mwangilwa's *Harry Mwaanga Nkumbula* (1982), and books on Zambian history have appeared, but there is no history of Zambia written by a Zambian.

Drama, on the other hand, has enjoyed a healthy existence. There have been two major influences on the development of theater in Zambia. One is the oral tradition of storytelling, which has maintained a widespread preference for what is seen and heard over what has to be read from the page. Another has been the British love of amateur theatricals, which led to the establishment by Whites of theater clubs in Lusaka, along the Copperbelt, and elsewhere,

WOMEN IN ART

Women artists face more difficulties than men because the idea of female independence conflicts with traditional values and disrupts the age-old social hierarchy in which women were expected to marry and become housewives. The village division of labor made women responsible for making domestic items such as pots, baskets, and mats, but though these were often works of art in themselves, their manufacture was seen as an element of household life and not as individual expression.

Although women today have as much right to an education in the arts as men, very few have made a mark as painters or sculptors. Men in general can tolerate a woman working—as a book illustrator, for example—but are opposed to their finding self-realization through artistic creation outside the traditional structures. Husbands find it particularly objectionable for wives to "exhibit" themselves on the stage, and most of Zambia's actresses are single.

Female musicians, singers, and dancers face even stronger opposition, and have now reacted by forming a pressure group called Women in Music, to strive for the right to follow the career that suits their talents. Women's position in the arts will become more prominent as they thrust themselves out of the constraints imposed by men who act as if the attitudes of the Victorian age in Britain should prevail forever.

often with a proper auditorium and the facilities needed for performances on stage. After independence these theaters came under the control of Zambians, and the heritage of the stage play has lived on.

Schools, the universities, colleges, and even the defense forces have drama groups, while parallel to the established theaters a number of clubs grew up which rejected their Britishness in favor of a post-colonial African approach to drama.

Plays by Zambian dramatists often deal with social problems (divorce and the laws of inheritance, for example) or historical topics—as in A.S. Masiye's *The Lands of Kazembe* (1973), and more recently with directly political issues such as corruption and power-hunger. Playwrights and performers are often recruited to tour the country to present didactic plays forming part of campaigns against, for example, AIDS.

A recent development is the video-taped television drama, broadcast in series such as "Play for Today" and "Play Circle." There is no film studio in Zambia, so these productions are made, usually with amateur performers, in borrowed houses, hospital wards, or school buildings, circumstances which impart to them a vivid naturalness. The plays often deal with highly

Opposite: **A *makishi* ("mah-kee-shee") dancer. Drama in Zambia has its roots in traditional story-telling, music, and dance.**

Until recently, Zambian publishers accepted only works that did not offend political or religious sensibilities.

A selection of crafts on display at the Kabwata Cultural Village.

controversial topics and some are rebroadcast time and again by popular demand. There are few professional actors and actresses in Zambia, and hardly any of the plays are printed and published.

CRAFTS

Even in the remotest villages, traditional craft items are being replaced by manufactured goods such as enamel saucepans and plastic buckets. In the urban areas the replacement is almost total. The craft heritage of Zambia's traditional culture is not, however, being allowed to fade away.

In the 1930s the Livingstone Museum was founded with the express objective of collecting and preserving what in those days was called ethnological material. The museum today has as fine a collection as anywhere else in Africa. Since independence, three other museums have enlarged the national collection—the Moto Moto Museum at Mbala in the north, the Nayuma Museum in the west, and the Tonga Museum in the south.

The government's Cultural Services Department manages centers where the skills to make the crafts are kept alive. In Lusaka, the Kabwata Cultural Village maintains the resources for men and women to make traditional items for sale. The museums also encourage the production of such objects and buy them for resale. Most of the crafts are bought by foreigners resident in Zambia or tourists. This market is also tapped by private entrepreneurs through shops in the major centers. Popular items are baskets, patterned reed mats, carved wooden bowls, baked clay pots, masks, shields, metalware, and musical instruments such as drums, hand pianos, and xylophones. There is considerable production of "airport art"—carved and polished wooden animals, birds, and human figures.

A modern urban craft is the making of model bicycles, cars, and aircraft, usually with moving parts, using steel or aluminum wire. Model bicycles have riders whose legs move up and down as if pedalling when the machine is propelled forward. These ingenious and skillfully made toys are often the work of children.

By buying Zambian crafts, tourists are helping to save them from extinction.

VISUAL ARTS

Traditional baskets, mats, wood carvings, masks, decorated pottery, jewelry, metal spearheads, combs, and axes were often of great beauty and made with a high degree of skill. But most of such works were utilitarian in purpose. The concept of visual art as a means of individual, rather than communal, creative expression is relatively new in Zambia.

Some Christian missionaries, if not the more puritanical churches, wanted devotional wood carvings and statues as well as paintings for their buildings, and this gave an opening to individual talent. In addition, Western secular education regards art as an essential part of the curriculum.

An art school was established in Lusaka shortly before independence, followed by the Department of Fine Arts at the University of Zambia, where persons who chose to be artists in the modern sense could receive training. Since then Zambia has produced dozens of fine painters and sculptors, some of them, however, self-taught. Much of these artists' work may be described as social commentary, particularly on the unequal distribution of wealth in the country or the trials of urban life in contrast to the simplicity of the rural past.

Few Zambian visual artists can earn a reliable living from their work alone. While some are well-known and popular there are at present few art galleries in business in the country which might provide the outlets they need, and few private Zambian collectors. Some artists sell from door to door, others exhibit in hotels and even private residences. Those who are in fashion may be fortunate enough to get commissions from banks and other corporations for paintings and sculpture, but the Lusaka International Airport terminal building, for example, does not feature the works of Zambian artists among its decorations, while the state's national art collection (even with its new national gallery) does not receive the funding to buy new work to any extent. The Lusaka art school was closed some time ago for budgetary reasons.

Despite the difficulties, which include the high cost of materials, Zambia's visual artists are producing an impressive variety of work. Individual talents differ, but the artists' creations are a mirror of society as well as the expression of individual genius.

Opposite: **Not many works of art would use soil, as this portrait by a Zambian artist does.**

THE HENRY TAYALI CENTER

The greatest artist of the modern period was the painter and sculptor Henry Tayali. Much of Tayali's work depicts the crowdedness of city life and the wish of the soul to transcend it.

The one-party state drew up a policy on the arts which intended to bind artists into a "socialist-realist" straitjacket like that imposed by Stalin on Russia, but Zambian artists revolted and founded their own Visual Arts Council (now part of the National Arts Council) to assert their independence. With the help of well-wishers, the VAC acquired premises for a workshop and gallery in Lusaka which has become the focus of activity in the visual arts. It is now called the Henry Tayali Center.

MUSIC AND DANCE

The most widely used musical instrument in Zambia is the drum, which comes in sizes 1.5–5 feet (0.5–1.5 m) tall and as wide as the diameter of the tree trunk from which it was made allows, with a membrane of leather. Drums in a sequence of sizes form a percussion orchestra to accompany singing and dance.

Another instrument which can be large and impressive is the xylophone. The keys are flat wooden strips tied to a wooden frame with gourd resonators, one beneath each key, in a succession of declining sizes from one end to the other. The keys are tuned to either an eight or a five-note scale, the former close to that which characterizes much Western music, and are struck with a rod topped with a ball of rubber.

The hand piano used to be a popular solo instrument. It consists of iron keys mounted on a small board, sometimes hollowed to form a resonator. The keys are adjustable so that they can be tuned. The hand piano is held between the hands and played with the thumbs. Today the homemade guitar, constructed with a tin can as resonator, is more often heard than the hand piano.

BODY ART

The earliest European travelers noted with admiration the care with which women dressed their hair to create stunning coiffures. This tradition has continued, and mothers today spend hours plaiting their daughters' hair and patterning it in intricate designs. Girls at school spend much free time doing this for each other, and many a young woman goes on to become a professional hairdresser, ambitious to open a salon of her own.

There are innumerable hair salons (sometimes called "saloons") in Zambia. Some of them are humble affairs in a thatched hut or under a tree, others as up-to-date as anywhere in the world, with all the equipment and unguents a lady of fashion might require.

A simple style may take only an hour or so to put into effect, but an elaborate creation may take half a day. Time passes quickly though, for the salon is not merely a place to have a head of hair turned into a work of art, but also a place for the exchange of news and gossip.

Other traditional instruments include rattles, reed flutes, horns, rasps, and the one-stringed harp. All the traditional instruments are used and taught at Maramba Cultural Village in Livingstone, and accompany the National Dance Troupe, which performs on state occasions and entertains at hotels and concerts.

Traditionally dance formed part of ritual ceremonies and much of that seen today has been adapted for the general audience.

Traditional singing is in choral form, with a lead voice to which the chorus responds. Solo singing, in the Western sense, is an innovation, and modern Zambian popular music, where the old instruments have given way to electric guitars, synthesizers and factory-made drum sets, is still basically choral as far as the singing is concerned. Individual star performers are rare. Among the young, American and British pop has a broader following than modern Zambian music. Zambian bands are strongly influenced by Western fashion. A characteristic of the Zambian audience is that it likes its music to be played very loud.

Above: **Hairdressing is an ancient art. This example is from the 19th century.**

Opposite: **A drummer performs at a cultural village.**

LEISURE

ZAMBIANS IN THE CITIES have a range of recreational activities to select from, but the choice depends on how much disposable income the person enjoys. Those who cannot afford to join sports clubs or the expensive equipment needed for most Western games are in much the same position as the rural poor, whose choice is very limited. Organized sport is a recent introduction to Zambia, as are facilities that depend on electricity, such as the cinema, radio, and television. In traditional life entertainment has to come from the resources of the village itself. Work could be enlivened with singing and dancing, while weddings are often the greatest opportunity to eat, drink, and have a good time.

Local festivals to celebrate the harvest or commemorate the ancestral spirits are enjoyable occasions, but the most regular form of entertainment is storytelling around the fire at night, with a pipe to smoke and beer to lubricate the proceedings.

POPULAR SPORTS

SOCCER Zambians—rich and poor, urban and rural —are united across all barriers by a passionate interest in soccer (also called football), while for anyone who can scrape together enough cash, the radio is as much a household item as a cooking pot.

Soccer is one of the sports in which Zambia excels. The game was brought to the country by the British, and was promoted by the mining companies as recreation for their workers. The earliest teams bore the names of mines, such as Bancroft Blades and Mufulira Blackpool. Over

Zambians amuse themselves by playing games like darts, draughts (*above*) and *nsolo* ("in-sorh-lorh," *opposite*). Many Zambians love to gamble.

A well-attended soccer match at the Lusaka Independence Stadium.

Zambia has produced not only Africa's best soccer team, but its most famous soccer commentator.

the years other business organizations encouraged the formation of their own soccer clubs, and the game has now reached the stage where Zambia has a fully fledged professional league. Many players who have become stars in Zambia are taken on by clubs abroad, in Europe, Saudi Arabia, South America, and South Africa. At home the game is governed by the Football Association of Zambia and internationally by the Federation of International Football Associations (FIFA).

It is from this environment that the country's national team is drawn, and that team is among the top three in Africa and among the world's top 20. The fortunes of the national squad are followed with almost religious devotion. Though it has yet to qualify for the World Cup, it has been close to doing so several times since 1974.

Zambia has also produced Africa's most famous soccer commentator, Dennis Liwewe, who since the 1970s has been the role model for others in the profession in many countries as a result of his broadcasts on the BBC. His son, Ponga, is following in his father's footsteps.

SOCCER—DISASTER AND RESURGENCE

The Zambian national team was well placed to get into the finals of the 1994 World Cup and on April 28, 1993 took off from Lusaka in a military aircraft to fly to Dakar for a qualifying match against Senegal. But it never arrived. Immediately after leaving Libreville, Gabon, after a refueling stop, the plane plunged into the sea. Eighteen players, 12 officials, and the entire aircrew perished, and Zambia lost the best soccer team it had ever had, and its captain, Wisdom Chansa.

When the news reached Zambia the next morning, people were so stunned that offices closed and crowds of mourners were weeping in the streets. But Zambian soccer has an inextinguishable spirit of its own, and within weeks a new team had been formed, with Kalusha Bwalya (pictured here), a star playing for a Dutch club, as captain.

Against all odds, Bwalya's team came within an ace of qualifying for the 1994 World Cup and winning the African Nations Cup, and was acknowledged to be the best team in Africa. It was as if the genius of the lost team had come back from the dead.

In Zambia a public subscription raised a large sum of money to provide for the families of those that had died in Gabon. The remains of the crash victims were buried adjacent to the Independence Stadium in Lusaka and a memorial erected. It has become a place of pilgrimage, and visiting teams go there to pay homage to the dead before their matches in the stadium.

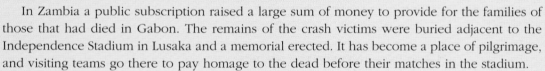

Zambia may be among the best in soccer, but it is a poor country. The Football Association is always short of money for the development of the game and the state's contribution to sport as a whole is small. The game extends from its central venue, the Independence Stadium in Lusaka, to every corner of the country, and Zambia also has one of the first Women's leagues in Africa. Being indisputably the national sport, even the barefooted play it, if only with a ball made with a bag stuffed with straw.

GOLF Another national game is golf, but it is confined to the better-off. Like soccer, it was introduced by the British to the mining towns and the administrative centers. It was for decades a pastime that could be enjoyed by Whites only on the many splendid links on the Copperbelt, in Lusaka and elsewhere.

But shortly before independence it was a Zambian, David Phiri, who became the first African to play golf for Oxford University, England, and win the acclaimed status of a Blue. When he returned home to work for the mines, the "color bar" crumbled, and then the game was given a great boost when it was taken up by President Kaunda. He laid out a nine-hole course in the spacious and elegant grounds of State House.

Kaunda is no longer president and his successor does not play golf but the presidential links is still maintained and is used mainly for prestigious charitable fund-raising tournaments. Zambia, with its first-class golf courses in the main centers, is on the international golfing circuit, and thousands of Zambians play the game regularly. Even small provincial towns have golfing facilities.

David Phiri, the Oxford Blue who ended race discrimination on Zambia's golf courses.

BOXING AND OTHER SPORTS Boxing has a large following, too, and Zambia has produced three Commonwealth champions—Lottie Mwale (light heavyweight), Chisanda Mutti (cruiser weight), and Joe Sichula (heavyweight)—with Joe Chigangu the current world junior heavyweight champion. In athletics, the hurdler Samuel Matete won a bronze in the 1996 Olympics.

Zambians also swim and play tennis, squash, hockey, rugby, and bowls, a game usually played on grass with large wooden balls. For those with a taste for adventure, whitewater rafting down the Zambezi gorges below the Victoria Falls makes the adrenaline flow, as does stalking big game as a licensed hunter in one of Zambia's game management areas.

Storytelling under the trees, with ample beer to quench the thirst.

RELAXING

A favorite way for Zambians to pass the time is, quite simply, conversation. Zambians are sociable people and enjoy storytelling, and—let it be said— gossiping, accompanied by the consumption of beer. In the rural village, the traditional meeting place is the *bwalo*. In urban areas, the bwalo is replaced by the tavern and the bar.

Missionaries and the colonial government tried, with some success, to turn Zambians into teetotallers, or at least to keep "European" liquor out of their reach. For many years the only legal public drinking places in urban areas were "beerhalls," usually owned by the local council. They were designed along the lines of a village social center, and the only liquor available was traditional beer marketed as Chibuku or Shake-Shake. After independence, beerhalls were renamed taverns, and continued to flourish.

Bars are places where all sorts of drinks are available. The most popular drink is bottled lager. Bars range in quality from cramped shacks in the

Beer has always been a part of Zambia's traditional culture. There is no temperance movement in the country, but a good number of people are abstainers for moral or religious reasons.

97

Above: **In both urban and rural areas, guitars made out of tins and boxes give hours of inexpensive entertainment.**

Opposite: **Listening to the radio in colonial days. (Oil on canvas by Stephen Kappata.)**

townships to expensive "Pleasure Resorts" where the bar is surrounded by gardens and there are thatched shelters against sun or rain. There is usually music from a stereo deck and, at weekends, a live band. People dance and may buy a meal of grilled steak, chicken, or sausages at a barbecue.

For persons with money to burn, there are more expensive pleasure centers in the cities, where they can find everything from a casino with roulette and blackjack to video games and a strobe-lighted dance floor.

There are few cinemas in Zambia, and they are all in the city centers. The wealthy do not go to the cinema at all, preferring a television set tuned to the world via satellite dish, or video films, which can be hired from the many video shops. Enterprising persons in the townships who are fortunate enough to have electricity establish their own mini-cinemas in their houses with a television set and video player.

Of all the electronic media, however, radio is the most popular, especially since the advent of the relatively cheap transistor run on batteries. A radio-cassette player can blast out music any time, and it is not unusual in the remotest places to see a herdsboy tending his livestock with a radio on his shoulder. Crowds gather around a radio set when a soccer match is being broadcast, and if its owner is a budding entrepreneur he may charge a small fee for listening.

Many people listen to foreign broadcasts in English. Radio South Africa, the Voice of America, and the British Broadcasting Corporation are popular, while the Netherlands, France, Germany, Japan, and Russia also have English services broadcast in Zambia.

WAYALESHI—THE SAUCEPAN RADIO

Radio or wireless (vernacular pronunciation "wah-yair-lair-shee") has had an important place in the life of the country since World War II, during which Zambian troops were serving in distant lands. At the time, communications within Zambia were poor, and many of the soldiers' families were unable to read. In order to keep the soldiers' loved ones informed of the progress of the war and of their men in arms, the government decided to distribute radios to the villages and the community centers in the towns. But standard radio sets were large, fragile, and expensive. The problem seemed insoluble until an information officer named Harry Franklin came up with a brilliant idea. In conjunction with the Eveready battery company in England, he designed a simple dry-cell battery set whose valves, circuits, and speaker fitted inside a small, tough saucepan.

The saucepan sets were distributed all over the country, and at the same time, Franklin set up Zambia's first broadcasting station in a prefabricated nissen hut at the airport in Lusaka (now called City Airport). This was the small beginning of the present Zambia National Broadcasting Corporation which covers the country with two shortwave and two mediumwave channels, and one FM and one television channel. Since 1991 three independent radio stations have also come on the air. Zambia's addiction to radio goes back a long time, while today the Saucepan Radio has become a collector's item.

Zambians who are literate love reading, and anyone who can, buys at least one newspaper a day. Sports, politics, and sex and witchcraft scandals are the most popular features, and someone will always be seen solving the crossword puzzle. Every newspaper has one, for solving crossword puzzles is another national obsession. Zambia's public libraries are few and far between, and new books are rare, but they are always full of readers. Few Zambians buy books because they are so expensive.

CHILDREN'S RECREATION

There used to be little organized recreation for children as they took part in the economic activities of their parents, who themselves had little recreation. Children grew up learning from their parents.

Now, in both rural and urban areas, boys and girls learn games at school, but after classes the girls usually stay at home with their mothers. Boys have more freedom, and as likely as not will be playing soccer on any open stretch of ground.

A netball practice at school. Netball is a game played by two teams of seven players, who are usually women.

Under the one-party state, youngsters were enrolled in the Young Pioneers, a state-controlled and highly politicized youth movement. It was disbanded in 1991. Today some young people join the Boy Scouts, Girl Guides, or similar associations organized by the churches. Worried by the large number of street children and the many others who do not have access to recreational facilities, the government has established a Ministry of Youth, Sport and Child Development.

NSOLO—A TRADITIONAL GAME

Nsolo is a game that moves at great speed, a game of skill that requires a good head for mental arithmetic. It can be played on a wooden board which has shallow holes scooped out of it in four parallel lines of eight, or on the ground, where holes are dug in the same pattern.

Two counters, which may be small stones, coins, nuts, or even bottle tops, are placed in each hole on the outside lines. The players face each other across the width of the board, and, starting on the left, move the counters toward the right in a complicated arithmetical succession. As the counters enter the second row, they can be captured by the opponent if he is able to place his counter next to it in his own second row. With this capture, he also takes the counters from any other hole he chooses. The game continues until one player has taken as many counters as possible, making it impossible for the opponent to continue.

A game between two experienced players on an 8 by 4 board can take as little as three minutes. But the board can be larger than that, up to 24 by 4, when the game is played by teams of three on each side. For the big game, the holes can be made on a long plank, on the ground, or on a raised concrete slab. A team game is noisy, with the counters clicking and the opponents taunting each other. Large sums of money are often staked on the outcome.

In urban areas, the game is played at taverns and bars by men and women. In traditional villages, it is played separately, the women's game having slightly different rules. Nsolo, under different names, is played all over Africa. Small portable wooden Nsolo boards can be bought in Zambia's craft shops.

Children are adept at making their own wire buses, motorcars, and bicycles. Many of these toys are sold to tourists.

FESTIVALS

ZAMBIANS ENJOY A NUMBER OF annual secular, religious, and traditional festivals and ceremonies. People of all faiths in Zambia celebrate their festivals and holy days freely.

In the national calendar Independence Day, October 24th, is the most important event of the year. In all cities of the Republic it is marked with parades, and special sporting events such as the finals of the Independence Cup soccer tournament and the national motor rally take place. Labor Day, May 1st, sees parades organized by the trade unions. It has become a tradition for employers to present long-service awards to workers on this day.

The first Monday of August is Farmers' Day, and the Zambia Agricultural and Commercial Show is held in Lusaka over that weekend. The show offers a fine display of Zambia's achievements in the farming sector and is a shop window for industrial products, with many Zambian and foreign

<table>
<tr><td colspan="2">PUBLIC HOLIDAYS IN ZAMBIA</td></tr>
<tr><td>New Year's Day</td><td>January 1</td></tr>
<tr><td>Youth Day</td><td>March 12</td></tr>
<tr><td>Good Friday</td><td>Variable</td></tr>
<tr><td>Holy Saturday</td><td>Variable</td></tr>
<tr><td>Holy Monday</td><td>Variable</td></tr>
<tr><td>Labor Day</td><td>May 1</td></tr>
<tr><td>Africa Freedom Day</td><td>May 25</td></tr>
<tr><td>Heroes and Unity Day</td><td>First Monday and Tuesday of July</td></tr>
<tr><td>Farmers' Day</td><td>First Monday of August</td></tr>
<tr><td>Independence Day</td><td>October 24</td></tr>
<tr><td>Christmas Day</td><td>December 25</td></tr>
</table>

Opposite: **The court bard sings the king's praises at the N'cwala ceremony.**

Left: **May Day parade.**

103

The royal barge is ready for the annual Kuomboka ceremony.

exhibitors. The show is usually opened by the president or a visiting foreign dignitary, who presents trophies to prize winners in categories that range from Best Beef Bull to Best Industrial Stand. The show is also a great occasion for fun, with music, a military tattoo, equestrian displays, and other entertainment. The Zambia International Trade Fair, held at Ndola on the Copperbelt in July, also offers a weekend of entertainment, apart from the serious business conducted between Zambian business people and the worldwide exhibitors.

The most important festival in Zambia's Christian calendar is Christmas. It is the time for the exchange of greeting cards and gifts, and some churches, such as the Anglican cathedral in Lusaka, host a charming Carols by Candlelight ceremony. Most industries in Zambia close down from Christmas Eve until after New Year, making this a holiday period. Christmas is commercialized in the style of Western consumer societies.

Although not designated public holidays, the Diwali of Hindus and Eid ul Fitr of Muslims are celebrated by these communities.

KUOMBOKA

Kuomboka means "to come out of the water," and signifies the greatest public ceremony of the Lozi, the heartland of whose kingdom is the floodplain of the Upper Zambezi. The Litunga has two capitals, one at Lealui on the plain, the other at Limulunga, on rising land on the east bank of the river. The Litunga and his court split the year between the two palaces. In March or April, when the rainy season has run its course, the plain becomes completely flooded, and Lealui is isolated. The Litunga must leave.

The Litunga in a procession during Kuomboka.

At the appropriate time, the royal drums are sounded, preparations are made, and the Litunga proceeds to the royal barge, the Nalikwanda ("nah-lee-kwahn-dah"). Propelled by skilled paddlers wearing scarlet berets, the great barge crosses the floodwaters and docks at Nayuma, the harbor on the shore. Crossing the water, Nalikwanda is followed by smaller royal barges and a flotilla of canoes.

Paddlers wearing red berets and print skirts move skillfully across the water.

The music of drums, xylophones, and singers accompanies the Litunga's procession, and his subjects wear their traditional Lozi costume, with its brightly colored long skirts. When the Litunga enters Nalikwanda at Lealui, he is dressed in his traditional robes, but during the journey he changes into a replica of the British admiral-of-the-fleet's uniform which was presented to his ancestor, Lewanika, when he attended the coronation of King Edward VII in London in 1902.

The origins of Kuomboka are hidden in the past, but the ceremony, as it now exists, though with a less grand barge, probably began, as the Lozi historians say, during the reign of Litunga Mulambwa in the 1820s. This was before the English started celebrating Christmas with Christmas trees. Kuomboka can be interpreted as the symbolic annual rebirth of the Lozi kingdom by its passage through water.

The days of the ceremony are a time of feasting for the Lozi and their guests, but the ceremony is not held if the Zambezi fails to flood because of drought.

LIKUMBI LYA MIZE

Mize is the place high up on the Zambezi plain where the Luvale royal chief Ndungu has his palace and occupies a throne guarded by statues of lions. *Likumbi lya Mize* means "the Day (in celebration of) Mize." It is held in September, the start of the planting season.

On that day, grounds near the palace become an arena into which come subordinate Luvale chiefs wearing splendid regalia to await the arrival of Ndungu, whose throne has been put in position at the head of the arena. Around the arena traditional Luvale artifacts are on show to remind people of their heritage. Baskets, knives, holsters, and other crafts are exhibited, but pride of place goes to the *lutengo* ("loo-tairn-gorh"), a working model of an ancient iron smelter, with demonstrations by a blacksmith in the art of making hoes and arrowheads. As the crowd waits, the arena is invaded by *makishi*, dancers wearing elaborate brightly painted masks and tightfitting costumes woven from differently colored fibers. They stand for the spirits, and dance the history of the Luvale in a thrilling display of gymnastics, accompanied by the insistent beating of drums.

Circumcision mask waiting to be donned by a *makishi*. Some costumes worn by *makishi* represent animals, such as a giant tortoise with a basketwork shell. Some *makishi* dance on stilts as high as 12 feet (4 m); others perform on ropes tied between tall trees.

When the time is ripe, Ndungu, wearing his crown and ceremonial robes, is carried in the royal hammock from the palace to the throne. The crowd pushes forward to catch a glimpse of him, because by tradition he lives in seclusion in the palace. When he is seated, a headman, his body decorated in red and ochre, and wearing a headdress of bright feathers, performs the royal dance *kutopoka* ("koo-torh-porh-kah"). The festival's climax comes as the court bard chants the history of the royal family, urging the spirits to assist the chief, and pledging the loyalty of his people.

Above: **Two Lunda subjects bow before Mwata Kazembe during the Mutomboko ceremony.**

Opposite: **Mwata Kazembe dances with sword and axe.**

In the old days during the Mutomboko ceremony a slave was sacrificed to symbolize the Mwata's victories. Today it is a goat.

MUTOMBOKO

Mutomboko is the Victory Dance festival of the Lunda of Mwata Kazembe, whose territory lies along the Luapula River in northern Zambia. Perhaps three centuries ago the first Mwata Kazembe broke away from the Lunda empire of Mwata Yamvo and crossed the Luapula River from the west into what is now Zambia, fighting and subordinating the people who stood in his way. Kazembe's capital, the town of Mwansabombwe, lies beside the Ngona River, a tributary of the Luapula. Mutomboko is celebrated here on July 29th each year.

The festival begins in the morning with the Mwata visiting shrines and paying homage to the ancestral spirits. Priests smear him with ochre and white sacred dusts, and he proceeds to the banks of the Ngona where he pours beer and throws food into the waters, saying "What your fathers died for should follow you." The ritual commemorates the drowning in the Lualaba River (in Congo) of two of the first Kazembe's brothers during the migration.

Members of the royal family, and chiefs and councillors in the Lunda hierarchy wear colorful traditional costumes and take their places in an arena. They are surrounded by a huge crowd watching the preliminary dances by girls, selected members of the royal family, and councillors. The Mwata, clad in his royal finery, modelled on a costume given to his predecessor in the 18th century by a Portuguese ambassador, and wearing his crown, which resembles that of the Mwata Yamvo, is borne on the royal hammock into the arena amidst great pomp and rejoicing.

The culmination of the ceremony comes when the Mwata rises, to deafening applause, and performs Mutomboko. He carries an axe and a sword, concluding his dance by pointing the sword to the sky (whence he comes) and then to the earth (where his body will rest). He thus unites the spirits and the people in his person. The king, followed by his wildly rejoicing subjects, is then carried back to his palace.

N'CWALA

Formerly suppressed by the colonial government, N'cwala is the First Fruits and Reinvigoration festival of the once warlike Ngoni of the Eastern Province. The ceremony centers on the ruler, at present Mpezeni IV, whose full title is Nkosi ya Makosi ("in-korh-see yah mah-korh-see"), King of Kings. In the past, the men of the Ngoni, an offshoot of the warrior Zulus of South Africa, were organized in *impi* ("eem-pee"), fighting regiments. N'cwala was the occasion for all to gather, be united through the king with the spirits, and be given renewed strength.

The ceremony, with its displays of war dancing, reaches its peak with the slaughter by hand of a black bull, which is then roasted on a spit. The first piece of cooked meat is eaten by the king, then all the warriors join in, the court bard chanting the praises of the monarch. At the appropriate time, the season's first fruits are presented.

N'cwala is a religious ceremony, and the ritual eating of the bull is symbolically similar to the Christian Eucharist. An Ngoni historian of N'cwala, M.B. Lukhero, comments that King Mpezeni's health and strength are identified with the well-being of his subjects and the fruitfulness of nature. His function at N'cwala is to bring back the departed spirits for the good of the people. The Zambian Ngoni are no longer warriors but farmers and cattle ranchers. While in the past the good of the people was achieved by conquest, today it comes from the soil, and the present ceremony is most concerned with food and the prosperity its abundance assures.

Today's participants in N'cwala dress in the leopard skins of warriors and dance with spears and shields, but the past glories are being ritualized. Though the sacred bull is eaten, so too are the first fruits of crops planted at the beginning of the rains, some four months previously.

The Ngoni celebrate their heritage in a dance of warriors during N'cwala. The festival is held each year in February or March, depending on the state of the harvest.

SHIMUNENGA

The Ila of Maala in the Southern Province, cattle people from the most ancient times, believe their ancestral founder to have been a leader named Shimunenga, who won them their territory by defeating his brother Moomba in battle. Shimunenga, after his death, did not live on as a mere spirit, but as a demigod. The Ila's most sacred place is Shimunenga's *isaka* ("ee-sah-kah"), a holy grove near the town of Maala, and he is commemorated annually in a three-day ceremony between September and November, this pastoral people's new year season. The exact date is decided by a direct descendant of Shimunenga, his guardian and priest.

The first day of the festival is the women's day. They go around the villages, dancing, singing, and drinking. The songs are vulgar and meant to provoke the men. On this day the men do nothing active except drink beer. On the second day the women pay homage to Shimunenga at his grove. Later everyone gathers at Chief Mungaila's palace. A sermon is given on Shimunenga's place in his people's lives and speeches are made, followed by singing and dancing until all are exhausted.

On the third day there is an awe-inspiring display of the Ila's best cattle. The herds, led by that of the chief, are stampeded in succession, to singing and the beating of drums. After the round-up the celebration of well-being continues with dancing and games, which include mock battles with real spears, and dramatized lion hunts. When it is all over around midday, the people, having paid homage and given thanks to Shimunenga for his beneficence, retire to drink beer, which is also a libation to the god.

Spectators to the Shimunenga festival are warned that to desecrate the sacred grove by entering it can bring dire consequences.

It is said that a reckless European who ignored the warning not to enter Shimunenga's holy grove died of a sudden illness a few hours after his intrusion.

111

FOOD

FOOD SECURITY is one of Zambia's major worries. The great drought of 1992 brought the country to the brink of starvation, from which it was saved only by swift and efficient government action with assistance from the United Nations and other agencies. About 300,000 tons of corn were imported and distributed in famine areas on the basis of a well organized Food for Work program. Not one person in the country died for want of food. Zambia faces a constant threat of grain shortage because it is so highly urbanized and no government has yet devised an effective policy for agriculture.

Corn, introduced to Africa by the Portuguese centuries ago, has become the staple food for most Zambians. Four other introduced starch crops—cassava, wheat, potatoes, and sweet potatoes—are also important. Before the arrival of these foods, the staple grains were the indigenous millet and sorghum and a little rice. Corn is ground and cooked with water to make a stiff porridge called *nshima* ("in-shee-mah"), or *nsima*, which can be eaten with the fingers.

Above: **Cooking *nshima*. Nshima is eaten with one or more side dishes, usually meat, fish, or vegetable stews.**

Opposite: ***Kapenta* being turned on drying racks.**

WOMEN AND FOOD

Most basic foods in Zambia are grown by women. In the traditional village, a woman not only spends much time in the fields, but also long hours preparing food. She has to collect firewood, carry water from the well or stream, and turn corn into meal by pounding it in a mortar or grinding it between stones. Cassava has to be soaked in water for a week to remove a poison, cut into chips, and dried before it can be made into flour.

Nowadays many villages have a small mechanical mill where grain is ground for a fee. In towns, factory-made meal is available in the shops and it is even possible to buy precooked nshima which is ready to eat when boiling water is added to it. In the urban areas, most of the food stalls in the markets or on the street are run by women. They usually sell nshima with grilled steak, chicken, or sausages, though more and more town people eat bread from the many bakeries and fried potato chips. Hamburger with chips is popular.

After preparing them at home, many a woman will go into the city center to sell a tray of hardboiled eggs, sausage rolls, deepfried doughnuts, or roasted peanuts. To a very large extent, it is women who keep Zambia fed.

ZAMBIAN SPECIALITIES

If carbohydrate nshima is the foundation of most Zambian meals, there are many protein foods to go with it. Those who can afford it will have beef, chicken, mutton, or pork, cooked in a variety of ways. One is plain grilling over a charcoal fire in a brazier called *mbaula* ("im-bah-ool-lah"). Another is in a stew containing onions and tomatoes. Herbs and spices are little used, and Zambian cuisine is generally bland.

Fish is also very popular, and comes from the country's many rivers, lakes, and wetlands. Fresh fish is transported from its source either packed in ice or in deepfreeze trucks. Much also comes to the markets sun-dried or smoked. The most widely eaten varieties are bream (tilapia), which are raised on fish farms as well, and *kapenta*, the freshwater sardine from lakes Tanganyika and Kariba.

Other protein foods include field mice, boiled or grilled on skewers like kebabs, and locusts, several types of grasshopper, tree caterpillars, and flying ants (termites)—all of which are roasted.

The flesh of wild animals such as antelope, buffalo, and hippo has always been part of the Zambian diet, but as hunting is regulated and for some species forbidden, such meat is now less common despite the activities of poachers. However, Zambia now has a number of game ranches, with the result that venison can be found in the shops—but it is expensive. Birds like guinea fowl, francolin, quali, doves, and pigeons also feed the pot.

Tilapia, or African bream, is bred in fish farms in many tropical countries in Africa and Asia. Tilapia is derived from the word tlape *from Botswana, where it was first encountered by Europeans.*

A rich variety of vegetables is sold in markets and on the streets.

Much use is made of vegetables such as cabbage, rape, and a wild spinach called *libondwe*, as well as okra, beans, and fresh or dried peanuts.

During the rainy season, the forests yield a bountiful crop of wild mushrooms, many of which are edible and have a unique flavor. In color they may be white, brown, scarlet, or bright yellow, and may look alarming to those who have only eaten cultivated mushrooms bought in a shop. Zambians cook their mushrooms in water or with a little oil. They can be added to meat and vegetable stews while some varieties are dried for future use. In the rural areas, they are sold by the roadside, though large quantities are brought to urban markets.

Tropical fruit like mangoes, pineapples, guavas, and wild plums from the forests are eaten daily when in season.

Many well-off Zambians have Western foods on their dining tables—cornflakes and bacon and eggs for breakfast, beans on toast as a snack, and roast chicken for dinner, but it would be unusual for there not to be one meal a day at which nshima was not present.

MARKETS AND SUPERMARKETS

Evidence of how productive the soil of Zambia can be is visible all year round in the markets in urban areas. There on offer are piles of tomatoes, onions, potatoes, cabbages, rape, eggplants, cucumbers, pumpkins, beans, bananas, oranges, and lemons. Beside the fresh produce stalls are others selling chickens, eggs, and fresh and dried fish. Visitors from cold climates always express surprise and delight at the freshness of Zambian fruit and vegetables and the full flavor of the meat, though the freshwater fish does not have quite the tang of that which comes from the sea.

In the brightly lighted air-conditioned modern supermarkets, customers find displays of every type of food. There is a butcher's counter with beef, lamb, pork, and perhaps venison, and freezers containing chicken and locally processed bacon, ham, and other meats, as well as Nile perch, *kapenta*, and bream. The dairy chests hold fresh pasteurized milk and cream, Zambian butter, cheeses, yogurt, and ice cream. There are half a dozen different types of bread as well as ready-to-cook snacks like

A woman serves her husband some traditional beer.

samoosas, spring rolls, and meat pies. In addition, the customer will find a wide range of imported foodstuffs, whether Greek olives, South African sea fish, or Chinese beansprouts. Zambians can eat well.

BEVERAGES

Traditional Zambian beer is brewed from millet, sorghum, or corn. Grain is first malted by being allowed to sprout, then dried. It is pounded into meal and soaked in water to ferment in several stages. The result is a slightly fizzy alcoholic drink. This beer is now also made in factories and called Chibuku ("chee-boo-koo").

In the North Western Province a strong mead, *mbote* ("im-borh-tair"), is brewed from the honey obtained in abundance from wild bees in the forests. Some people add sugar to the corn brew to give it a higher alcohol

content, and distill the product using a homemade apparatus of pipes and a cooling bath. The result is a potent spirit called *kachasu* ("kah-chah-soo"), which is illegal and dangerous to drink.

There is a large market in Zambia for bottled lager, and two industrial breweries, in Lusaka and Ndola, produce several brands of different strengths. Wine is made on a small scale from grapes and other fruit. A firm in Lusaka blends various brands of brandy, gin, whisky, and vodka, but these products do not compare in quality with those imported from South Africa or Europe.

Tea and coffee are not widely consumed except in offices, though Zambia produces tea and a fine arabica coffee, much in demand abroad, especially in Germany. The most popular nonalcoholic drinks are carbonated products such as Coca Cola, Pepsi, and Fanta.

A favorite traditional nonalcoholic drink is munkoyo *("moon-korh-yorh"), a sweet "beer" of which the wild tuber of that name is an ingredient.*

Cooking is often done outdoors in rural areas.

DINING OUT IN LUSAKA

Lusaka, both the capital and business center of Zambia, also has a large diplomatic corps, and many tourists passing through. Many restaurants of international standard cater for this and the local clientele, and typically for this part of Africa, many of them are steak houses where Zambian beef is grilled to perfection. Apart from these, Chinese, Indian, Pakistani, Lebanese, Greek, and Italian cuisines can be savored, while the large hotels regularly feature the Zambian menu.

Of special note is the restaurant at the lodge in a game ranch only 30 minutes' drive from the city center. The restaurant is so renowned that tourists on the railway safari between South Africa and Tanzania stop there for a meal and a drive around the park. A feature of the menu is venison, prepared in interesting ways that satisfy the most discriminating palate.

TRADITIONS AND ETIQUETTE

It is not generally customary for Zambians to invite guests to their homes. Westerners may find this disconcerting and see it as a sign of unfriendliness. But that is not the case at all. Zambians expect friendly persons to call on them unannounced.

They will be treated as honored guests, and immediately offered a drink and a snack. If mealtime is approaching the visitor will be asked to join in. It is customary to cook more food than needed for the family, just in case visitors should arrive.

NSHIMA WITH PEANUT CHICKEN

(Serves 4–5)

3 cups finely ground cornmeal
1 teaspoon salt
6 cups water
3 lb (1.4 kg) chicken
salt to taste
4 cups (about 1 liter) hot water

$1^1/_2$ cups roasted peanuts, brown skins removed, or $1^1/_2$ cups roasted salted peanuts with the salt washed off
1 large onion, chopped
1 sweet potato, about 8 oz (225 g), peeled and left whole

Mix cornmeal, salt, and water until there are no lumps. Bring to a boil slowly, stirring with a wooden spoon until porridge is thick and cooked (about 15 minutes). Place in a serving bowl, cover, and keep warm.

Wash and cut chicken into neat pieces. Leave the breast meat on the bone. Boil the chicken and salt for 30 minutes with 1 cup water. Pound peanuts to a powder. Mix the powder with 3 cups hot water and add it to the chicken after it has been boiling for 30 minutes. Add onion and sweet potato.

Continue to cook gently until the chicken is done, about an hour, or more if the bird is tough.

Zambian food is bland, and cooks may like to add pepper or chili, powdered or whole, while the dish is cooking.

Nshima is the same thing as the Italian polenta. Leftovers can be cut into slices, dipped in egg, and fried in oil to make fritters.

Peanuts, a favorite food, are sold on the street. *Chikanda* ("chee-kahn-dah") is a soft cake made with peanut flour and the wild *chikanda* tuber, which gives it a special flavor and a bright pink color.

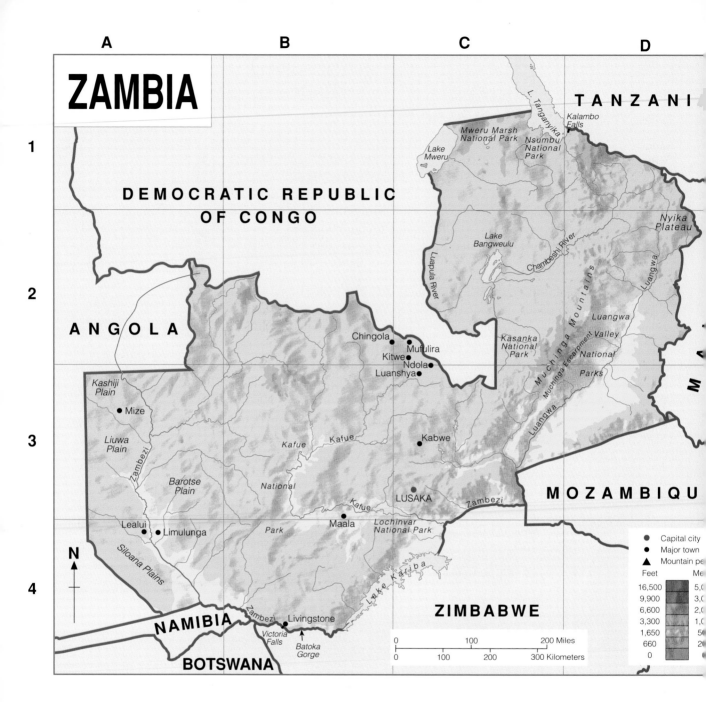

ZAMBIA

DEMOCRATIC REPUBLIC OF CONGO

TANZANI

ANGOLA

MOZAMBIQU

ZIMBABWE

NAMIBIA

BOTSWANA

L. Tanganyika

Kalambo Falls

Mweru Marsh National Park

Lake Mweru

Nsumbu National Park

Nyika Plateau

Luapula River

Lake Bangweulu

Chambeshi River

Muchinga Mountains

Luangwa

Luangwa Valley

Kasanka National Park

Muchinga Escarpment

National Parks

Chingola

Mufulira

Kitwe

Ndola

Luanshya

Kashiji Plain

Mize

Liuwa Plain

Kafue

Kafue

Kabwe

Zambezi

Barotse Plain

National

LUSAKA

Zambezi

Lealui

Limulunga

Maala

Kafue

Lochinvar National Park

Park

Siloana Plains

N

Zambezi

Livingstone

Victoria Falls

Batoka Gorge

Lake Kariba

●	Capital city
●	Major town
▲	Mountain pe

Feet	Me
16,500	5,0
9,900	3,0
6,600	2,0
3,300	1,0
1,650	50
660	2
0	

0   100   200 Miles

0   100   200   300 Kilometers

A   B   C   D

1

2

3

4

Angola, A2

Bangweulu, Lake, C2
Barotse Plain, A3
Batoka Gorge, B4
Botswana, A4

Chambeshi River, C2
Chingola, B2
Congo, Dem. Rep. of, B1

Kabwe, C3
Kafue National Park, B3
Kafue River, B3
Kalambo Falls, D1
Kariba, Lake, B4
Kasanka National Park, C2
Kashiji Plain, A3
Kitwe, C2

Lealui, A4
Limulunga, A4
Liuwa Plain, A3
Livingstone, B4
Lochinvar National Park,
  B4
Luangwa River, C3, D2
Luangwa Valley National
  Parks, D2
Luanshya, C3
Luapula River, C2
Lusaka, C3

Maala, B3
Malawi, D2
Mize, A3
Mozambique, D3
Muchinga Escarpment, C2
Muchinga Mountains, C2
Mufulira, C2
Mweru, Lake, C1
Mweru Marsh National
  Park, C1

Namibia, A4
Ndola, C2
Nsumbu National Park, C1
Nyika Plateau, D2

Siloana Plains, A4

Tanganyika, Lake, C1
Tanzania, D1

Victoria Falls, B4

Zambezi River, A3, B4,
  C3
Zimbabwe, C4

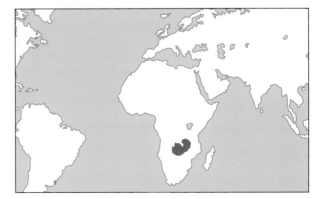

QUICK NOTES

OFFICIAL NAME
Republic of Zambia

LAND AREA
250,000 square miles (750,000 square km)

POPULATION
9.4 million (1996 estimate)

CAPITAL
Lusaka

PROVINCES
Lusaka, Central, Copperbelt, Eastern, Northern, Luapula, North Western, Western, Southern

NATIONAL SYMBOL
African fish eagle

NATIONAL FLAG
Dark green oblong with vertical stripes of black, red, and copper forming a square in the bottom outside corner, surmounted by copper eagle with outstretched wings.

MAJOR RIVERS
Zambezi, Chambeshi, Luapula, Kafue, Luangwa

MAJOR LAKES
Tanganyika, Kariba (manmade), Mweru

HIGHEST POINT
Nyika Plateau (above 7,000 feet/2,300 meters)

LANGUAGES
Official: English
Semiofficial: Bemba, Kaonde, Lozi, Lunda, Luvale, Nyanja, Tonga

RELIGIONS
Catholic and Protestant Christianity, traditional beliefs, Islam

CURRENCY
Kwacha. K1,300 = US$1.00 (June 1997)

MAIN EXPORTS
Copper, cobalt, gemstones

IMPORTANT ANNIVERSARIES
Independence Day (October 24)

LEADERS IN POLITICS
Harry M. Nkumbula, (1917–82), founder of Zambian nationalist movement
Kenneth Kaunda (1924–), President 1964–91
Frederick J.T. Chiluba (1943–), President 1991–

LEADERS IN LITERATURE
Stephen Mpashi
Andrea S. Masiye
Dominic C. Mulaisho

IMPORTANT TRADITIONAL CEREMONIES
Kuomboka (March–April)
Likumbi lya Mize (September)
Mutomboko (July 29)
N'cwala (February–March)
Shimunenga (September–November)

GLOSSARY

(NOTE: Words in Zambian languages bear no stress. There are no diphthongs, and each vowel is spoken separately.)

Bantu ("bahn-too")
People.

Batwa ("baht-wah")
Small people, that is, Pygmies.

bwalo ("bwah-lorh")
Village meeting place.

Chibuku ("chee-boo-koo")
Factory-made traditional beer.

chikanda ("chee-kahn-dah")
A soft cake.

kachasu ("kah-chah-soo")
Illicit distilled alcohol.

kapenta ("kah-paint-ah")
Sardine-like fish.

Kuomboka ("koo-orhm-borh-kah")
Lozi ceremony, meaning to come out of the water.

kwacha ("kwah-chah")
Zambian currency.

Lesa ("lair-sah")
God the Creator.

libondwe ("lee-borhn-dwair")
Wild spinach.

lobola ("lorh-borh-lah")
Bride price.

mandevu ("mahn-dair-voo")
Beards.

mbote ("im-borh-tair")
Honey beer or mead.

MMD
Movement for Multi-Party Democracy, the present ruling party.

Mosi Oa Tunya ("morh-see wah toon-yah")
Zambian name for Victoria Falls.

munkoyo ("moon-korh-yorh")
Wild tuber used in making sweet beer.

Mutomboko ("moo-torhm-borh-korh")
Victory dance festival of the Kazembe Lunda.

N'cwala ("in-chwah-lah")
First Fruits and Reinvigoration festival of the Ngoni.

nshima ("in-shee-mah")
Thick corn porridge.

nsolo ("in-sorh-lorh")
Traditional game played with counters and two or more rows of holes on a board or on the ground.

Shimunenga ("shee-moo-nairn-gah")
Ancestral founder of the Ila of Maala.

UNIP ("yoo-neep")
United National Independence Party, in power 1964–91.

wayaleshi ("wah-yair-lair-shee")
Wireless; radio set.

BIBLIOGRAPHY

Chan, Stephen. *Kaunda and Southern Africa*. UK: I.B. Tauris, 1991.

Hamalenga, Munyonzwe. *Class Struggle in Zambia and the Fall of Kenneth Kaunda*. Lanham, MD: University Press of America, 1992.

Johnson, Walton R. *Worship and Freedom: A Black American Church in Zambia*. Ann Arbor, MI: Books on Demand, 1977.

Livingstone, David. *Letters and Documents: The Zambian Collection*, ed. T. Holmes. Bloomington, IN: Indiana University Press, 1990.

Prins, Gwyn. *The Hidden Hippopotamus*. New York: Cambridge University Press, 1980.

Roberts, Andrew. *A History of Zambia*. New York: Holmes & Meier Publishers Inc., 1976.

Ter Haar, Gerrie. *Spirit of Africa: The Healing Ministry of Archbishop Milingo of Zambia*. Lawrenceville, NJ: Africa World Press, 1992.

Vaughan, Richard and Murphy, Ian (illustrator).*Zambia*. USA, 1992.

(With thanks to the Librarian, The American Center, Lusaka, Zambia.)

INDEX

African National Congress, 26, 32
agricultural festivals, 103–104, 107, 109–110
agriculture, 10, 11, 13, 27, 42–43, 53, 60–61, 66, 103, 113
AIDS, 50, 68–69, 74, 85
ancestral worship, 9, 93, 105, 108, 110–111
Angola, 7, 28, 37, 45
art, visual, 88–89
"Asians," 53, 75
Atlantic Ocean, 7, 8, 23

banking, 46
body art, 91
Botswana, 7, 40, 115
Britain/British empire, 23, 24, 25, 77, see also colonial rule
Broken Hill Man, 19
bwalo, 61, 97

Bwalya, Kalusha, 95

cattle, 11, 42, 43, 59, 60, 110, 111
Chansa, Wisdom, 95
Chigangu, Joe, 96
Chiluba, Frederick, 29, 33, 71
China, 23, 45
Christianity/Christians, 23–24, 33, 50, 57, 58, 59, 64, 65, 71–75, 83, 104,see also Christians, missionaries
churches, 16, 36, 68, 71, 73–75, 100, 104
cities, 14–17
  Kabwe, 15, 19, 40
  Kitwe, 15, 66
  Livingstone, 15, 16, 17, 91
  Lusaka, 10, 14, 15, 16, 17, 26, 28, 33, 34, 37, 45, 46, 55, 65, 66, 68, 74, 75, 77, 81, 84, 87, 88, 94, 95, 96, 99, 103, 104, 119, 120
  Ndola, 15, 40, 46, 66, 72, 104, 119

civil service, 29, 31, 66
clans, 51–52, 55
climate, 10
Coillard, François, 24
colonial rule, 15, 24–26, 32, 50, 52, 53, 71, 77, 83–85, 93, 95, 97, 105, 109
communications, 16, 45
Congo, Democratic Republic of, 7, 20, 37, 40, 77, 78, 108
constitution, 31–34, 53, 71, 77
copper, 3, 20, 22, 23, 25, 27, 39, 40–41
Copperbelt, 15, 25, 35, 41, 46, 65, 84, 96, 104
Copperbelt University, 66, 67, 81
corn, 42, 43, 113, 115, 118, 121,see also nshima
crafts, 83, 86–87, 107
crime, 37, 69

INDEX

cultural villages, 83, 86–87, 91
currency, 20, 39, 46, 65

dance, 74, 83, 85, 90, 93, 98, 107, 108–109, 111
defense/defense forces, 29, 37, 77, 85
diplomatic relations, 36–37
drinking/drinks, 93, 97, 111, 118–119
drought, 10, 40, 43, 61, 106, 113
Dupont, Henri, 24

economic reform, 39, 44, 60–61
education, 27, 58, 61, 64, 66–67, 68, 71, 75, 80, 81, 85, 88, 89, 100
elections, 26, 29, 33, 35, 36, 43, 53, 78
environmental issues, 12–14, 46
Ethiopia, 15, 36
exports, 42, 44

family customs, 57, 58
family planning, 50, 74
fauna, 8, 12–13, 15, 19
Federation, 26–27
fish, 12–13, 47, 115, 117
flora, 10, 11
football, 35, 93–95, 98, 100, 103
Franklin, Harry, 99
fruit, 116, 117, 119
funeral customs, 59

games, traditional, 101, 111
golf, 95–96

health, 27, 61, 63, 68–69, 75, see also AIDS, infant mortality
Hindus, 75, 104
holidays, 103–104
housing, 57, 61, 62
human rights, 34
hydro-power, 8, 10, 13, 40

independence, 15, 16, 27, 31, 32, 42, 53, 66, 71, 77, 85, 86, 88, 96, 97
India, 23, 31, 51, 53, 69, 75
Indian Ocean, 7, 8, 23
industry, 40, 53, 104
infant mortality, 50, 58
initiation rites, 58

Islam, 75
ivory, 22, 23

kapenta, 13, 113
Kapwepwe, Simon Mwansa, 26, 27
Katilungu, Lawrence, 26
Kaunda, Kenneth David, 26, 27, 28, 29, 32–33, 35, 43, 53, 55, 60, 66, 71, 84, 96
Korsten Basketmakers, 74
Kuomboka, 104–106

lakes:
    Bangweulu, 8, 12
    Kariba, 8, 13, 22, 47, 115
    Mweru, 8
    Tanganyika, 7, 9, 12, 47, 79, 115
land control, 53, 60, 72
languages:
    Bantu, 72, 78, 79
    Bemba, 78, 79, 80, 81
    English, 77–78, 79, 80, 81, 84, 98
    French, 77, 81
    Kaonde, 78
    Lingala, 78
    Lozi, 78, 80
    Lunda, 78
    Lungu, 79
    Luvale, 78, 79
    Nyanja, 78, 79, 81
    official, 77–78
    Portuguese, 79
    semiofficial, 78, 80, 81
    Swahili, 77, 78, 79
    Tonga, 51, 78
    Zulu, 21, 78, 79
life expectancy, 50
Likumbi lya Mize, 105, 107
literacy, 27, 84
literature, 80, 83–86
Livingstone, Dr. David, 17, 20, 23–24, 47, 73
Liwewe, Dennis, 94
Lunda-Luba empire, 49, 78
Lusaka: see cities

makishi, 85, 107
Malawi, 7, 45, 75
manufacturing, 44
markets, 117–118
marriage customs, 51, 57, 58–59
Masiye, A.S., 85

Matete, Samuel, 96
mining/mines, 3, 15, 20, 29, 39, 40–41, 50, 53, 66, 93, 95, 96
missionaries, 23–24, 50, 64, 71, 72, 73, 80, 83, 88, 97
Movement for Multi-Party Democracy, 29, 33, 35, 39, 43
Mozambique, 7, 8, 22, 28, 37, 45, 77
Mulaisho, Dominic C., 84
museums, 17, 47, 86, 87
mushrooms, 11, 116
music, 74, 83, 85, 90–91, 93, 98, 104, 106, 111
    traditional instruments, 90–91
Muslims, 50, 75, 104
Mutomboko, 105, 108–109
Mutti, Chisanda, 96
Mwale, Lottie, 96
Mwangilwa, Goodwin, 84

N'cwala, 103, 105, 109–110
Namibia, 7, 28, 37, 40
national parks, 3, 11, 12, 46
    Kafue Park , 8, 13
    Kasanka Park, 12
    Lochinvar Park, 12
    Nsumbu National Park, 12
    South Luangwa National Park, 8, 12, 13, 47
newspapers, 80, 100
Nigeria, 20, 78
Nkumbula, Harry Mwaanga, 26, 32, 84
Northern Rhodesia, 15, 17, 19, 24, 26
nshima, 113, 114, 116, 121
nsolo, 93, 101

one-party state, 29, 31, 32–33, 34, 35, 39, 74, 83, 89, 100, 105
orphans, 33, 68

people:
    Afro-Asians, 52
    Afro-Europeans, 52
    Bantu, 20, 51
    Batu-Batotwe, 51
    Batwa, 51
    Bemba, 21, 24, 51, 52, 81
    Chewa, 21, 49, 50
    Chokwe, 51
    Ila, 105, 110–111

Kaonde, 51, 81
Kololo, 21, 23, 78
Lenje, 51
Leya, 14
Lozi, 14, 17, 21, 24, 49, 50, 81,
    105–106
Luba, 20
Luchazi, 51
Lunda, 14, 20, 21, 24, 49, 51, 105,
    108
Luvale, 51, 81, 105, 107
Mambwe, 51
Maravi, 21
Namwanga, 51
Ngoni, 21, 24, 49, 50, 51, 52, 78,
    105, 109–110
Nsenga, 51
Nyanja, 81
Portuguese, 22, 23, 28, 108, 113
San, 19, 20, 51
Soli, 51, 55
Swahili, 22, 23
Tonga, 81
Tumbuka, 51
Whites, 15, 24, 25, 26, 32, 52, 53,
    61, 65, 84, 96
Zulus, 109
Phiri, David, 96
police, 29, 37, 77
political parties, 35, see also African
    National Congress, Movement for
    Multi-Party Democracy, United
    National Independence Party
population statistics, 14, 15, 16, 50,
    58, 62, 66, 67, 68
president, eligibility, 33
proverbs, 81

racial discrimination, 15, 25, 52, 96
radio, 78, 93, 98, 99
railways, 15, 16, 45, 61
religion, traditional, 72, 73, 83
Rhodes, Cecil John, 24
rivers:
    Chambeshi, 8, 79
    Kafue, 8, 11, 12
    Lualaba, 8
    Luangwa, 7, 8, 23
    Luapula, 8, 14, 21, 108
    Zambezi, 7–8, 11, 14, 17, 19, 21,
        22, 23, 24, 79, 96, 105, 106

rulers, traditional, 53, 21, 24, 53, 55, 60,
    64, 72
    Chitimukulu, 21, 51
    Lewanika, 24, 106
    Litunga, 14, 21, 24, 50, 105–106
    Mpezeni I, 21
    Mpezeni IV, 109, 110
    Mpezeni, 24, 51
    Mungaila, 111
    Mwata Kazembe, 14, 21, 24, 51, 108–
        109
    Mwata Yamvo, 21, 108
    Ndungu, 107
    Sebitwane, 21, 23
    Zongendaba, 21
Second Republic, 32
Shimunenga, 105, 110–111
Sichula, Joe, 96
slavery, 22, 23, 24, 55, 71, 75, 77, 108
South Africa, 17, 21, 25, 28, 37, 40, 45, 49,
    53, 65, 69, 74, 78, 94, 109, 119, 120
Southern Rhodesia, 19, 26, 27, 28, 37
sports, 93–96, 103
storytelling, 83, 84, 85, 93, 97

Tanzania, 7, 77, 120
Tayali, Henry, 89
television, 78, 85–86, 93, 98, 99
theater, 84–85
Third Republic, 31, 33
tourism, 17, 46–47, 83, 87, 120
trade fair, 46, 104
trade unions, 26, 29, 33, 36
trade, early, 22–23

United National Independence Party,
    26, 27, 29, 32, 33
United Nations, 36, 37, 113
United States, 31, 33, 42, 74
University of Zambia, 16, 66, 67, 81, 88

vegetables, 116, 117

waterfalls:
    Kalambo Falls, 9, 12
    Kundalila Falls, 40
    Victoria Falls, 7, 13, 14, 17, 19, 40, 47,
        79, 96
wayaleshi, 99
women, 35, 36, 37, 42, 57–59, 64–65, 85,
    91, 95, 111, 113–114

World War II, 25, 99
writing, 80

Zanzibar, 23
Zimbabwe, 7, 8, 14, 15, 19, 28, 37,
    40, see also Southern Rhodesia
Zion Apostolics, 74

PICTURE CREDITS

Elizabeth Blackwell Elementary